Vietnamese Cooking

Quick, easy, delicious recipes to make at home

The Essential **Asian** Kitchen

Vietnamese Cooking

ROBERT CARMACK   DIDIER CORLOU   NGUYEN THANH VAN

PERIPLUS

First published in the United States in 2003 by Periplus Editions (HK) Ltd., with editorial offices at 364 Innovation Drive, North Clarendon, Vermont 05759 and 130 Joo Seng Road #06-01/03 Singapore 368357.

© Copyright 2003 Lansdowne Publishing Pty Ltd

Library of Congress Cataloging-in-Publication Data is available.
ISBN 13: 978-0-7946-5031-5
ISBN 10: 0-7946-5031-7

DISTRIBUTED BY

North America, Latin America
& Europe
(English Language)
Tuttle Publishing
364 Innovation Drive
North Clarendon, VT 05759-9436
Tel: (802) 773-8930
Fax: (802) 773-6993
Email: info@tuttlepublishing.com
www.tuttlepublishing.com

Japan
Tuttle Publishing
Yaekari Building, 3rd Floor
5-4-12 Osaki, Shinagawa-ku
Tokyo 141-0032
Tel: (03) 5437-0171
Fax: (03) 5437-0755
Email: tuttle-sales@gol.com

Asia Pacific
Berkeley Books Pte. Ltd.
130 Joo Seng Road
#06-01/03 Singapore 368357
Tel: (65) 6280-1330
Fax: (65) 6280-6290
Email: inquiries@periplus.com.sg
www.periplus.com

Commissioned by Deborah Nixon
Text: Robert Carmack
Recipe Consultants: Didier Corlou, Nguyen Thanh Van
Photographer: Louise Lister
Stylist: Janelle Bloom
Designer: Bettina Hodgson
Production Manager: Sally Stokes
Project Coordinator: Bettina Hodgson
Editors: Carolyn Miller, Susin Chow
Food Assistant: Chris Sheppard
Stylist for pages 18, 106, 107: Robert Carmack
Photographer and stylist for endpapers: Vicky Liley
Props: Market Imports Pty Ltd, Mrs Red & Sons, Origin Homewares
       Village Living @ Avalon, Room by Room Homewares

Set in Spartan Classified on QuarkExpress

Printed in Singapore

10 09 08 07 06   8 7 6 5 4 3 2

Note regarding Vietnamese translations throughout this book
Regional terminology and dialects vary throughout Vietnam. When the book lists two Vietnamese translations for the same word, the first indicates the northern expression, as used in and around Hanoi; the second indicates the southern expression, as used in and around Ho Chi Minh City (Saigon).

Contents

Introduction

My family has always lived in Hanoi, and I grew up there in a house of nine—four girls, two boys, plus my parents and grandmother. But times were not always easy, especially as my father was in the military and often far away from our family. Yet even during times of hardship both my grandmother and mother proved wonderful cooks. They comforted our hunger with delicious morsels, and when the cupboards were bare, they countered with frugal family recipes. Later, when my sisters were old enough to learn to cook, I became their star pupil: I mastered the art of eating! It was then that I developed a love of food that has carried me through to my present position of sous-chef at Hanoi's oldest and most prestigious hotel, the Metropole. Originally, I began as a translator in its multilingual kitchen: French, English and Vietnamese. It was a dream come true, for not only could I use language skills honed at university, but I also wore an apron. Straight away, I found myself so attracted to the job that I put my whole heart and soul into it. And today, I feel a special pride in presenting my country's authentic Vietnamese dishes to the people of so many foreign lands.

—Nguyen Thanh Van

History and geography

Vietnam is a long, narrow country, stretching more than 1,025 miles (1,650 km) from north to south—about the size of Japan, or slightly smaller than California. It has a population of just over 73 million, with almost three-quarters rural folk, although its "baby dragon" economy is rapidly transforming it from an agrarian society into an industrialized one.

The country's shape is fittingly comparable to two laden rice baskets on either end of a carrying pole, with its narrowest point a mere 30 miles (45 km) from east to west. It consists of three geographical regions: the northern Red River delta, the mountainous Annamite coastal range in the middle, and the southern Mekong delta, known locally as the Song Cuu Long or "River of Nine Dragons." Geographically, Vietnam is bordered on the east by the South China Sea, on the west by the Gulf of Siam, Cambodia and Laos, and on the north by China. While the country is covered inland with lush forest, the densely populated regions along the coast and deltas are awash with dykes, canals and waterways; the vast Mekong estuary, for example, extends over some 23,000 square miles (36,000 sq. km). Vietnam is a veritable land of water, as personified by one of the country's cultural exports, water puppets, which are carved mannequins that glide effortlessly over a watery domain and are "invisibly" manipulated by actors who stand in a blackened pool of water.

Mythologically speaking, the Vietnamese, or Kinh people, originated from the union of the mountain princess Au Co with the dragon lord Lac Long Quan. Indeed, the craggy rock formations of picturesque Ha Long Bay ("Descending Dragon Bay") are reputed to be the matrimonial bed. The beginning of Vietnamese nationalism started with the shedding of China's one-thousand-year rule, which lasted from 111 B.C. to 939 A.D. During the ensuing millennium, until French colonization in the mid-nineteenth century, Vietnam grew both in size and influence. Its southern neighbor Champa, once a state so strong it challenged the mighty power of Cambodia's Khmer Empire, was eventually obliterated by Vietnamese conquest. Throughout this time, Vietnam maintained the status of an independent tributary state to China, yet its internal affairs were zealously guarded. And despite periodic partitioning between competing political family dynasties, the ideal of a politically undivided Vietnamese union survived. Nevertheless, China continued to influence all aspects of Vietnamese culture—unlike neighboring countries, including the Champa kingdom, where Indian-based art forms, written language and government prevailed. From China, Vietnam adopted an appreciation for the arts and architecture, as well as its written language, and Confucian government and societal organization. (Officials even dressed similarly to Chinese mandarins.) Likewise, in religion it adapted China's Mahayana sect of Buddhism.

In the mid-nineteenth century, Western powers laid claim to great swaths of the area, with Vietnam, Cambodia and eventually Laos all falling under French domination, and becoming unified under the name Indochina. It was also during this time that the Roman or Latin alphabet replaced Chinese characters in Vietnam's written language; until then, Vietnam had maintained its unique language system that incorporated Chinese script in both pronunciation and pictograms.

Under French colonization, the country's agriculture was ruthlessly transformed to rubber and sugarcane farming, and scarce land for rice cultivation became even more prized. Japan's World War II occupation saw Western servitude transformed into Eastern bondage. (To some degree, the French Vichy government was considered an ally, and consequently French colonials were allowed freedom until the collaborationist government's fall, after which all French colonials were imprisoned.) Some 1 million Vietnamese died of starvation during this period, as Japan shipped away the country's entire rice production to feed its own islanders. Another thirty years of war ensued, first from 1945 to 1954 when the French attempted to reassert its control of Indochina, and afterwards with the ensuing partition of the country at the seventeenth parallel into North and South Viet Nam. It is believed that a further 3 million people perished between 1954 and 1975, until the fall of Saigon and the reunification of the country. Years of isolation and impoverishment followed until 1986, when Vietnam warily opened its doors with the introduction of doi moi ("renovation"), slowly transforming this communist country into a market economy.

Culinary history

Vietnam's cooking is a fusion of the best culinary elements. In the kitchen, China's traditional influence shows in the use of chopsticks and woks, plus stir-fried dishes and a plethora of noodles. The cool winter climate of Hanoi lends itself particularly to soups and stews of Chinese parentage, and steamboat fondues, known as lau, of Mongol descent. In all parts of the land, grilled foods, cooked directly over charcoal or rice chaff, are popular, especially in signature dishes like bun cha.

From 1802 until the end of World War II in 1945, the city of Hue, near the center of the country's north–south axis, served as the nation's imperial capital, although the French administrative headquarters were in Hanoi. Here, street food is chili-spicy, while restaurant fare remains richly influenced by the former court. Imperial cuisine is characterized by small portions in multiple courses, each progressively more artistic, and a bias toward vegetarianism. (While Buddhism does not proscribe the eating of animals, killing is anathema to Buddhists.) Local specialties include banh khoai, a smaller version of the rice starch and coconut-milk crepe known as banh xeo in Saigon, and bun bo hue, a noodle soup redolent of citronella.

Foods from the torrid south are typified by the old rhyme "sugar and spice and everything nice." It is a tropical cuisine enriched not only by the spice trade of neighboring kingdoms, but also by the generous use of sugar in savory dishes. Likewise, the popularity of soupy curries—with and without coconut milk—betrays an Indian influence. Because the southern Vietnam has large post-war diasporas, this is the style of cooking Westerners are most familiar with. Lingering aspects of French culinary influence include a fondness for baguettes and sandwiches, filtered coffee (often heavily sweetened with condensed milk), and dishes such as crème caramel—although made with coconut milk—and orange (or pineapple) duck. In the kitchen, the flat-bottomed frying pan has challenged Asia's ubiquitous wok. But it is arguably the integration of French ingredients with Vietnamese techniques that leaves the most indelible mark. For Vietnam's fresh markets literally groan with Western vegetables like potatoes, carrots, tomatoes, cauliflower, cabbage and asparagus (which interestingly is translated as "Western bamboo shoots"). And it was the French who nurtured a taste for beef, not only in stir-fries and braises, but in what could be described as the country's best-known national dish, pho bo noodle soup.

All of Vietnam is particularly ablaze with fun and activity for the lunar new year's Tet celebrations, or Tet Nguyen-Dan. Akin to Chinese New Year, Tet is also a time to pay homage to the kitchen hearth deity, Tao Quan, who yearly presents the family's "report card" to the heavenly Emperor of Jade. Festivities last anywhere from three days to two weeks, and it is a time of "out with the old" and "in with the new" when families reunite to share food and presents. Homes are scrubbed clean, then adorned with peach and apricot blossoms representing good fortune and peace. Pairs of watermelons are purchased for the home, with the deep red flesh indicating special luck throughout the year. Adults exchange gifts such as quality tea leaves, kumquat trees, sugared ginger and sweetened coconut, plus special foodstuffs like banh chung, a sticky-rice cake stuffed variously with sweetened pork and mung beans, wrapped in banana leaves and boiled for eight hours. Children are given bright red envelopes, or "li xi," filled with cash. While firecrackers were once ubiquitous during the celebrations, they have since been banned by government decree. Another popular holiday is Tet Trung Thu, or Mid-Autumn Festival, held in the eighth lunar month, when the moon shines brightest. This is the time to buy sweet moon cakes filled variously with lotus seeds, sesame seeds or mung beans. The rice harvest festival of Tet Lua is held in May or June. While birthdays are not traditionally celebrated, ancestors are honored on the anniversary of their deaths and this is known as Ngay Gio. Here, a veritable buffet traditionally groans with four dishes of each kind, from soups to noodles to desserts, plus suckling pork.

The Vietnamese diet

It is no coincidence that the Vietnamese word for steamed rice, com, is the same as the word for meal. As in other countries of East Asia, rice is more than the daily bread: it is the meal's focus. But, while Vietnam ranks as the world's third leading rice exporter, and some 60 percent of the land is devoted to rice, its quality is not rated as highly as Thailand's or America's. As in Thailand, the preferred steamed rice here is jasmine. Though similar to the standard long-grain rice grown around the world, jasmine boasts a fragrant, slightly floral

smell. Markets sell quantities of various rices, from the freshest new season's crop, labeled AAA, to "old" rice, which actually commands a premium price. Like much of Asia—with the notable exception of Japan—Vietnamese consumers appreciate the special qualities and taste of aged rice. Cooks claim it absorbs more water, thus swelling to a greater volume, but most of all is easier to cook. New rice, by contrast, tends to turn mushy or sticky during cooking. In a Vietnamese market, look closely at the selection and note the pristine white hues of fresh rice, graduating to the subtle parchment tinge of older rice. Broken grains (which are often preferred for cooking into a morning porridge or gruel) decrease the cost. Rice suited for grinding fetches even lower prices.

As befits a country where this grain is the daily bread, the variety is seemingly infinite. In some regions, particularly among the hill tribes of the north, sticky (glutinous) rice (gao nep or xoi) is the mainstay, and the basis for the famous Tet New Year's cake served throughout the country. More

chalky in appearance than standard rice, sticky rice is soaked for hours prior to steaming over water. As its name implies, it clings solidly. Likewise, black sticky rice is also popular. The rice is actually deep purple, and although it is usually soaked then steamed, it is also sometimes boiled to make a porridge-like pudding. It is often sweetened.

Besides rice grain, a vast array of rice noodles is ever-present, from the thin rice vermicelli noodles known as bun, which are eaten unheated, to the wider and more resilient banh pho noodles, the same as those used in the country's national soup dish, pho. Thin sheets of rice paper are softened and commonly used to wrap cooked meats at the table, or are filled to make both fresh and fried spring rolls.

Your first step to creating a successful Vietnamese meal is to frequent an East Asian grocer. Chinese stores are probably the most common, but you can also seek out Thai, Indonesian and especially Vietnamese family-run establishments that sell local specialties. Familiarize yourself with their wares, then trek wider to Indian stores and even natural foods stores for other products. But don't let ingredient unavailability deter you. Substituting ingredients is how fusion food begins and new cookery trends continue. Common mint suits most dishes that traditionally use other herbs, and canned coconut milk is almost as good as—and certainly more convenient than—fresh. If sour, unripe fruits are unavailable, substitute tart apples. Pungent fish sauce reigns supreme in Vietnamese cooking, but fermented yellow bean sauce or even diluted soy sauce is its vegetarian equivalent. While Vietnamese cooking is much less spicy than, say, Thai food, if there is intolerance to hot food, remove all the seeds from chilies. Luckily, mild finger-thick chilies are the norm in Vietnam.

While the esoterica of tropical fruits, vegetables, herbs and spices appears daunting, the ready availability of Asian ingredients nowadays makes cooking ever easier. Even herbs such as perilla (rau tia to), Vietnamese mint (rau ram) and piper leaves (la lot) can be found in the ethnic markets of Paris, Seattle and Sydney. A range of unusual herbs and lettuces is important at the table, for they not only make for adventurous eating, but also have medicinal qualities. These greens are rich in vitamins and minerals, and provide dietary fiber.

As for "seafood," the term is not a good description of Vietnam's aquatic bounty. There is a decided preference for freshwater fish, with their finer flake and sweeter flesh (but often with "muddy" undertones). Overseas, ex-pat Vietnamese fishmongers receive weekly deliveries of air-freighted freshwater fish, especially catfish, filling the void in countries relying primarily on saltwater varieties. More unusual offerings include snails, frog and eels. In terms of meat, pork and chicken dominate the menu, although duck is also hugely popular. Beef is still relatively pricey owing to the scarcity of grazing land. Nevertheless, due to France's long colonization, this meat has become firmly entrenched in the diet. Surprisingly, organ meats (offal) such as intestine and heart fetch a higher price than fillet! As also befits a nation so heavily influenced by China, anything that walks or squirms appears fair game. Northern Vietnam is just as notorious for its dog butcheries as it is for its "traditional" restaurants that serve an exotic range of animals and serpents, from cobra to monkey to porcupine.

Preparing a Vietnamese meal
It is said that the Vietnamese won "the American War"—their term for the long and costly Vietnam War between 1965 and 1975—with fish sauce and bicycles: in other words, with protein and mobility.

And there is some truth to the adage, for a Vietnamese meal can be as humble as rice with fish sauce, or nowadays more simply a large bowl of steamed rice, a cauldron of soup, and a generous platter of lettuce leaves and herbs, plus nuoc cham dipping sauce.

The main dinner meal is usually consumed at home, and consists largely of the same: rice, herbs and nuoc cham, plus several dishes from fried fish to simmered or braised meat, and soup. The Vietnamese use a yin-yang approach when combining dishes: that is, they marry cold with hot, soft with crunchy, dry with wet, and bright with bland. They also vary the ingredients, not repeating the same meats or flavors. Harried cooks will value the fact that preparing a Vietnamese meal does not mean precise timing from stove to table. Although soups are served piping hot, and stir-fries generally are cooked to order, many other dishes are commonly served warm or at room temperature. Except at a royal banquet, there are no distinct courses in a Vietnamese meal, and when dishes are served they can be consumed in any order.

When eating a Vietnamese dinner, do not accumulate several different dishes on your plate at once. Rather, fill a small bowl with steamed rice, then place a spoonful of any one of the dishes onto the rice. (When using chopsticks, use the top blunt end to grab communal food.) Bring the bowl to the mouth and eat that dish with some rice, before starting on a different dish. Soup is regularly spooned atop the rice to moisten it and, at the end, any remaining broth is poured into bowls and all rice is finished, for it is considered a bad omen if even one grain of rice is left.

Some Western tourists find it perplexing when sitting down to a meal in Vietnam that the Vietnamese eat with chopsticks (although Chinese-style soup spoons are the norm for watery broths). Even more surprising for them is the number of dishes eaten with the hands. Lettuce and herb leaves are regularly used to enfold pieces of cooked meat, as are various rice noodles and rice papers, thin egg omelets, and pancakelike crepes. The importance of fresh greens as part of a meal, including a plethora of fresh herbs, cannot be stressed enough. Like the ubiquitous, seasoned fish sauce table condiment, nuoc cham dipping sauce, these are *de rigueur* at the Vietnamese table.

As in other Asian countries, desserts per se don't exist and sweet confections are rarely served at the end of a meal. Instead, fresh fruit is likely to be proffered. More commonly, sweets are taken with afternoon tea or as between-meal snacks, such as the sweetened soupy che. Examples range from sugary beans mixed with crushed ice to chilled sweetened condensed milk with agar agar jellies. The Vietnamese trek to street cafes and market food stalls anytime during the day, until well after the evening meal, to partake of such treats.

While dinner is the day's mainstay, lunch and breakfast dishes also include foods that may seem formidable to the Western stomach. But, unlike at dinner, these are more likely to be single-dish offerings, and not an array of choices. A typical breakfast dish is pho, a rice noodle soup embellished variously with cooked or raw beef, cooked chicken or sometimes seafood. As with other meals, it is accompanied by fresh herbs, plus table condiments of choice, from sugar to fish sauce and chilies to vinegar. This breakfast dish originated in Hanoi, and is consumed well into the night, although scornful southerners jibe that northern cooking is so bereft of variation that locals have to eat breakfast all day long! Rice congee, or porridge, and boiled rice in water are both breakfast dishes but are strongly of Chinese origin.

Standard lunch dishes include steamed broken rice with a bit of meat, fried rice and pickles, and grilled meat or fish with fried glass noodles.

Treat dips, sauces and other condiments as you would, say, mustard, ketchup and relish in the West, or the array of chutneys accompanying an Indian meal. These side dishes complement many dishes, but not everyone will like pickled onions with their silky pork sausage—or conversely, steak sauce on their meat. But one thing is certain: all Vietnamese will want nuoc cham sauce at the table, as well as a veritable array of table seasonings, from granulated white sugar to chilies in vinegar and chili sauces both hot and sweet. Soy sauce, by contrast, is offered to tourists, as the Vietnamese cater to the belief that fish sauce's pungency may offend visitors. Sadly, poor-quality soy sauce is the norm in Vietnam.

As for beverages, plain water and hot water are the standard accompaniments, but, for additional nutrition, the rinse water from vegetables is also drunk, rarely being discarded. During a meal, a glass of local wine similar to sweet vermouth, beer or rice wine may also be drunk. After the meal, everyone consumes semi-fermented tea, often imbued with jasmine or lotus blossom. It is usually served hot in the north, and sometimes iced during summer months, but it is commonly chilled year-round in the sweltering south. Other popular beverages include juice extracted from sugarcane, sweet lemon or lime sodas, soy milk and che, a sugary iced soup of various beans and jellies, or sometimes young corn, sticky rice or lotus seeds. But again, these beverages are not usually drunk at mealtime. The country also brews its national beer, "33," for both local consumption and export, plus various local brews throughout the country. Of special note is bia hoi, or "fresh beer," which is never served in a tourist haunt, as it is relegated to

the locals. The locals have it delivered daily, and, at its best, it is a lemony-fresh palate cleaner and highly recommended.

You would think that, after one hundred or so years of French colonization, wine would have left a permanent stain on Vietnam's psyche. Surprisingly, dry European-style wine is far from common, although new international joint ventures close to the coastal city of Nha Trang have table grapes growing from the coast to the terraced highlands of inland Dalat. When drinking wine with Vietnamese food, don't restrict white wine only to seafood dishes, and don't subscribe to the belief that, with Asian food, sweet or spicy wines are preferable to dry varieties. French Riesling and un-oaked Semillon are best. Also, try any number of low-tannic reds such as a French Côtes-du-Rhône or a Bordeaux (claret). Hearty Spanish-style wines are less successful. Or, choose New World Pinot Noir, Grenache or Cabernet Sauvignon.

Equipment

Brazier or hibachi grill (lo nuong than hoa), grilling racks and chimney coal starter The Vietnamese regularly grill their foods over small braziers imbuing the foods with charcoal smoke. The traditional charcoal brazier works on the same principal as a chimney coal starter: stoked from the bottom, using newspapers and/or kindling, with coals resting above on a central rack. Once lit and covered with a white ash, the coals are ready for use. **Note:** Do not attempt to grill atop the chimney coal starter. Once fully lit, transfer the coals. Any Western grill (barbecue) can also be used or, more typically, a small Japanese-style hibachi. Both lava rock or ceramic briquette grills and indoor fan-forced grills can substitute, but they will not imbue the food with the same smoky flavors. (Make sure to use natural lump charcoal and not briquettes; see page 18.) Likewise, an oven broiler (grill) or a ridged grill pan is an alternative for apartment dwellers. Small, hand-held lattice wire baskets (vi nuong/kep cha) allow foods to be securely caged for easier turning and are convenient pieces of equipment.

Coffee filter, teapot, tea cozy (phin pha ca phe/am pha che/am pha tra am gio) Essential to a traditional kitchen is a small teapot, usually firmly ensconced in a tea cozy to retain warmth. Typically, the brew is made early and left to steep all day, with more hot water added with each cup. The most common tea is a semi-fermented green tea, often imbued with jasmine or lotus flowers. It is drunk plain, never with milk or sugar. Coffee is made strong, by slowly dripping hot water through an espresso grind. The metal filter cup, phin pha ca-phe, is typically placed atop a small bistro glass

Considering the complexity of Vietnamese food, the simplicity of a Vietnamese kitchen comes as a surprise. You'll find little more than a couple of charcoal braziers or gas rings, a frying pan or wok, a pair of scissors or shears, and some earthenware pots. Bowls and the ubiquitous rice cooker round out the picture, plus a slab of wood to serve as the chopping board. A wide curved-edge cleaver is essential for chopping, but Western-style knives will suit for all other tasks. Outside of that, a modern food processor easily replicates the monotonous pounding required to make Vietnamese meat pastes, such as for silky pork sausage, or to pulverize shallots and chilies in nuoc cham sauce. Traditionalists may choose to use a mortar and pestle.

Central to a Vietnamese home is the hearth and, one week before the annual Tet Festival, offerings are given to the kitchen deity Tao Quan. This lunar New Year celebration is a time for extravagant food preparation, still done in the traditional way. As in other parts of Southeast Asia, most of these tasks—from pounding to grinding and even washing—are done while squatting on a tiled floor.

Steamed rice is central to Vietnamese meals, hence the rice pot—or more appropriately a thermos-like rice container—holds center stage. With today's ever-rising affluence, the electric rice cooker has found greater popularity. But while steamed rice is now commonly cooked in an electric rice cooker, sticky (glutinous) rice requires traditional methods. Unlike steamed long-grain rice, which is boiled, sticky or glutinous rice is steamed over water, never actually touching the liquid.

Just as stock or broth is fundamental to Western cooking, homemade coconut milk is central to southern Vietnamese cooking. Coconut graters used to be a mainstay, but grated coconut for milk is just as likely today to be purchased from the local market to make fresh coconut milk on the spot when needed. Traditional coconut graters are shaped like a small stool, designed so that the cook can sit and then straddle the grater to rub half a coconut shell against the spiked end of the grater. Smaller hand-held models are more the norm today.

Traditional brazier (lo nuong than hoa), grilling rack and coal starter

Hibachi grill

Coffee filter, teapot, tea cozy (phin pha ca phe/am pha che/am pha tra am gio)

Mortar, stone (coi da) and pestle (chay)

Steamboat or fire pot (noi lau)

Wok, shovel and brush (chao ran/chao xao/xeng xuc)

Mortar, stone (coi da) and pestle (chay) A large stone or pottery mortar and pestle are best, as ingredients are wont to fly out of small, wooden Western-style models.

Steamboat or fire pot (noi lau) Variously called Mongolian hot pots and steamboats, Asian "fondues" are round, doughnut shaped vessels, with a central heat source. The food is cooked in a hot broth at the table. The steaming broth is the source for the name steamboat, while firepot takes its name from the smoking center chimney filled with hot coals.

Wok or frying pan, shovel and brush (chao ran/chao xao/xeng xuc) Both flat-bottomed skillets and round-bottomed woks are the frying pans of Vietnam. Nonstick Teflon-coated frying pans are useful. As for woks, use any standard sheet-iron wok from an Asian shop, although it must be seasoned to prevent rust and sticking. Food in heavier, coated cast-iron woks tends to stick uncontrollably. Woks work best over gas rings, allowing the flame to lap over the sides. Electric woks, while convenient, may not register high enough heat. Wooden and metal shovels are designed with a rounded end, facilitating scraping along the contours of the wok. For nonstick surfaces, however, use only wooden or plastic implements such as large palette knives, spatulas and pancake turners. Never scour a wok with soap (see page 19), and use only a plastic or other non-metallic brush.

1

2

3

4

Step-by-step how to prepare a brazier

1. Charcoal is best lighted outdoors directly in the brazier or hibachi (see Caution). To light coals, mound a small pile of charcoal atop a central rack. Tightly wrinkle newspapers and/or kindling in its base, and set newspapers alight. If using a special chimney coal starter (as shown on page 17), do not use kindling. Alternatively, mound a small pile of charcoal around an electric fire starter, plug in, and after 7 minutes remove starter.

2. Once coals are covered with a layer of white ash, spread them evenly in the brazier or hibachi using tongs or a small shovel. If using a chimney coal starter, spill the lit coals onto the center grate of the brazier. Slide the air vent at the bottom open to stoke the coals; for lower heat, close the vent.

3. Place grill rack (or grilling rack basket) on brazier and heat. To prevent sticking, hold a piece of fat with tongs and rub it along the grids. Alternatively, brush lightly with oil.

4. When cooking soups and stews on the brazier, comfortably nestle terracotta pots or a wok atop coals. Fan the coals and open all grill vents to increase heat while cooking.

Notes: Lump or natural charcoal is preferable to charcoal briquettes, as it is pure, and burns at a higher temperature. Avoid instant lighter liquids, fire sticks and other chemical fire agents, as these may produce unpleasant fumes at the table. Never use gasoline or kerosene, as both are dangerously explosive.

Any outdoor grill (barbecue) can be used in place of a brazier or hibachi.

Caution: If burning any form of charcoal indoors, always ensure that the room is well ventilated. Otherwise, carbon monoxide poisoning may occur.

Step-by-step how to
season a new wok

1. Place the dry wok over high heat. Wipe lightly with oil and heat until smoking. Immediately plunge the wok into hot water, then return to heat to dry. Wipe again with oil and repeat these steps a total of 3 times. At no time should you use soap.

2. When cooking with a wok, always preheat it before adding any ingredients, including oil. After adding oil, rotate the wok to spread it around the inside, then heat oil before adding any food. Because of the wok's conical shape, a gas flame is preferable to electric, as it disperses the heat upward along the sides of the wok. Gas also allows instant regulation of the heat.

3. To keep the wok clean, plunge into hot water immediately after use, scouring with a plastic or nonmetallic brush. Never use soap, as this requires you to season all over again. Do not wipe dry; rather place wok over a low flame to dry. Wipe lightly with oil and store. If you do not have a wok, use a large, seasoned cast-iron or nonstick frying pan, or a heavy saucepan or pot.

1

2

3

Arrowroot (bot dao/cu dao tinh)
Because of its cheaper cost in Vietnam, arrowroot is more popular than cornstarch (cornflour) for thickening sauces. Unlike cornstarch, arrowroot thins after boiling.

Bean sauce (bean paste) (tuong), commercial Fermented soybeans ground with water, salt and roasted rice powder. Look for a Vietnamese or Thai brand, as Chinese varieties are sweetened. Alternatively, use whole brown soybeans in brine, drained and mashed to a paste; do not confuse with Chinese fermented black beans, or recipe on page 114.

Beans, dried (pulses) (do/dau)
Dried beans, often served sweetened, are much smaller than Western pulses: black beans and green mung beans are about the size of standard lentils, black-eyed peas (beans) only slightly larger. Substitute dried azuki beans or Indian pulses, such as black gram.

Chili sauce, Asian (tuong ot) Asian chili sauces, such as Vietnamese or Thai, are slightly thick, bright orange-red in color, and made with crushed chilies, vinegar, garlic and sugar. Chili sauce is a standard table condiment in Vietnam, both in soup and with grilled meats. Do not substitute Tabasco, unless you decrease its quantity to a few drops.

Fish sauce (nuoc mam) Made from the fermented extract of salted small fish, or sprats, naturally brewed, acrid-smelling fish sauce is the mainstay of Vietnamese cookery. It is used both in the kitchen and as a table condiment, especially when diluted and combined variously with lemon, chilies and sugar to make the ubiquitous nuoc cham dipping sauce. Vietnamese- and Thai-style fish sauces differ slightly. (See Glossary, page 122.)

Ingredients

Use these pages as an aid to identifying common Vietnamese ingredients, from dry goods and sauces, to spices, fresh fruits and vegetables, fresh herbs for the table and various noodles.

Also refer to the Glossary (pages 122–124) for information on other ingredients.

Arrowroot (bot dao/cu dao tinh)

Bean sauce (bean paste) (tuong)

Beans, dried (pulses) (do/dau)

Chili sauce, Asian (tuong ot)

Fish sauce (nuoc mam)

Rice, long grain (gao te)

Rice starch (bot gao)

Seaweed, Vietnamese dried (rau cau)

Seaweed, Asian dried

Shrimp, dried (tom kho)

Shrimp sauce (mam tom/mam ruoc)

Rice, long grain (gao te) The principal rice used in Vietnamese cuisine is long-grain jasmine rice (gau tam thom), although sticky (glutinous) rice (gao nep/xoi) is also popular. Rice is the mainstay of the Vietnamese diet, and no meal is complete without its presence, either as rice noodles or steamed grain. (See Glossary, page 123.)

Rice starch (bot gao) Various varieties of Asian rice starch (which, confusingly, may be labeled "rice flour") are made from the amylose, or soluble portion, of both sticky (glutinous) and standard white rice. Unlike ground rice flour, rice starch feels silky to the touch. Bot gao te/bot be tinh khiet, made from standard white, long-grain rice, is the basis for batters like ban xeo crepes. Bot gao nep, or sticky (glutinous) rice flour, is the base for a myriad of dumplings, cakes and doughs; do not use to thicken sauces. (See also page 97.)

Seaweed, dried (rau cau) Vietnamese seaweed or moss comes variously in gray to tan color, and is extremely thin, like angel hair. There are also thicker generic Asian dried seaweeds or algae. Do not confuse with Japanese seaweed, such as wakame, which is much thicker. Soak before using, and rinse very well for grit.

Shrimp, dried (tom kho) Small dried shrimp make a quick base for soup. Soaked briefly in warm water and drained, they can be added to a myriad of dishes, from stir-fries to salads.

Shrimp sauce (mam tom/mam ruoc) Although they differ in thickness, northern Vietnam's mam ruoc and its southern counterpart, mam tom, differ in thickness. Both are extremely pungent. Substitute a premium Chinese shrimp sauce or Western anchovy paste.

Cardamom, brown or black (thao qua) Large oval pods, about 1 inch (2.5 cm) long, with a ridged brown exterior, tasting slightly of camphor. Use whole to flavor soups, such as pho. Known also as "bastard" cardamom. Crush lightly to expose its sticky black seeds, adding both pod and seeds to soups and marinades. Remove the pod when grinding with other spices. Do not confuse with the miniature, Chinese-lantern-shaped cardamom pods used in Indian cooking.

Chili (ot), fresh and powdered Vietnamese food is not particularly fiery, although fresh and pickled chilies are served at the table to season dishes individually. Long, mild, finger-thick chilies are most common (use, for example, Anaheim). Medium-length chilies (for example, Serrano) flavor dishes with more heat, and are used especially in the southern and central regions. As the seeds are the hottest part of the chili, remove them to decrease piquancy. The tiny ot chi thien/ot hiem chili (like Pequin) is the hottest. Ground chili powder is also popular, especially in the south.

Cinnamon Cinnamon and cassia bark are very similar, and can be interchanged. It is used ground, and sometimes in stick form.

Cloves Like cinnamon, this flavors five spice powder, and is used as a fragrant spice.

Curry powder Turmeric usually dominates Vietnamese blends, and in some cases can be used in place of the blended powder. Any mild Indian or Southeast Asian curry powder can substitute, although some Vietnamese blends contain less of the anise and cumin flavors.

Spices (cac gia vi kho) The five basic spices of northern Vietnamese cooking are black pepper, star anise, cinnamon, ginger powder and the large pods of brown cardamom. Southern Vietnamese cooking favors cloves, chili powder and curry powder or dried turmeric.

Cardamom, brown or black (thao qua)

Chili (ot), fresh and powdered

Cinnamon

Cloves

Curry powder

Ginger (gung), fresh and powdered

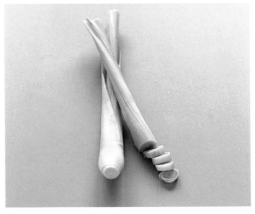

Lemongrass (sa)

Pepper, black

Star anise (hoi)

Turmeric (nghe and bot nghe)

Ginger (gung), fresh and powdered A beige- to golden-colored rhizome. Older ginger is more fibrous, yet pungent. During summer, look for tender young ginger for garnishes, such as in julienne strips. It is identifiable by its thin, parchment-like skin. Ground dried ginger is also popular, especially in the south.

Lemongrass (sa) The tough, green leaves, or shoots, of citronella-like lemongrass both color drinks and flavor tea, while the bottom one-third of the stalk, the white portion, is of principal culinary worth. To store, stand upright in 1 inch (2.5 cm) water and refrigerate for up to 2 weeks.

Pepper, black and white Black pepper is liberally used in northern Vietnamese cooking and more common than white. It is regularly sprinkled atop cooked dishes—meat and especially vegetables alike—just before serving.

Star anise (hoi) An eight-pointed pod with an aniseed flavor. When ground is a major component of five-spice powder. Use whole.

Turmeric (nghe and bot nghe) Fresh turmeric (nghe) is a rhizome that grows underground. It is grated, then soaked. Both the soaking water and pulp are used. (Caution: Wear gloves when preparing fresh turmeric, as it can stain.) For ground dried turmeric (bot nghe), if possible choose the darker Alleppey variety, instead of the milder Madras turmeric. Its flavor is closer to the fresh rhizome.

Banana flower (hoa chuoi) The tender inner petals are eaten both cooked and raw. (Discard the sticky immature banana shoots when peeling back the petals.) Soak the petals in acidulated water to prevent discoloration and to tenderize.

Banana leaf (la chuoi) The ubiquitous presence of banana plants in Southeast Asia makes this a natural choice for wrapping food parcels. Wipe leaves before using. To soften prior to folding, run briefly over a gas flame until the milky or waxy underside becomes shiny. Alternatively, use plastic wrap or aluminum foil.

Bean sprouts (gia) Fresh mung bean sprouts taste strong with age, so buy them fresh daily and rinse before using. Better yet, quickly blanch in boiling water, then soak in ice water until crisp. Purists remove both bean and hairlike tail, using only sprout stem.

Carambola (star fruit) (khe) A star-shaped fruit, eaten both unripe with Table Greens (see page 50) or used as a souring agent in soups and stews, or fully ripened as a sweet snack. Technically, there are two kinds: a yellow variety, and its more sour green cousin.

Coconut (dua) Young coconuts (dua non), identifiable by a green husk, or a thick, white fibrous shell that has been hacked clean, are exported frozen to Asian and Pacific markets. They come laden with a refreshing water and a jellylike flesh. Older coconuts (dua gia), with hard brown shells, are common at most Western supermarkets. Grate their firm flesh for myriad uses, from extracting coconut milk and cream to fresh and dried (desiccated) coconut meat.

Fruit and vegetables Fresh, sweet fruit crowns the end of a Vietnamese meal, but underripe or green fruits and vegetables are commonly used to give a distinctive tang to Vietnamese dishes. When unavailable, add lemon juice or tamarind puree.

Banana flower (hoa chuoi)

Banana leaf (la chuoi)

Bean sprouts (gia)

Carambola (star fruit) (khe)

Coconut (dua)

Cucumber (dua chuot)

Leek (toy tay)

Lettuce (rau xa lach)

Lotus leaves (la sen)

Lotus seeds (hat sen)

Cucumber (dua chuot) Standard Ridge, or "American," cucumbers are about 8 inches (20 cm) long and 2 inches (5 cm) thick, dark green in color, with a shiny skin. The seeds and peel are generally removed before eating. English (hothouse/telegraph) cucumbers can be substituted.

Leek (toy tay) Both baby- and standard-sized leeks are used, but only the white section. Substitute whole scallions (green onions). Sweet pickled "leeks" (cu kieu) are made with various ingredients from miniature leeks or scallions and are available at Asian grocers. These are a common table accompaniment.

Lettuce (rau xa lach) Soft lettuce leaves, such as red leaf (coral/Lollo Rossa), oak leaf and especially butter or Boston lettuces (rau diep), are essential to the Vietnamese meal, along with sprouts and assorted herbs. Crisp iceberg or head lettuce is less popular.

Lotus leaves (la sen) Large, voluptuous leaves from the aquatic lotus plant. These are commonly used to wrap foods, imbuing a slight chestnut flavor to various dishes. Fresh lotus is available from May to September in Vietnam, but dried leaves are more commonly sold overseas.

Lotus seeds (hat sen) Slightly resembling chickpeas, dried lotus seeds are commonly added to soups and stews for a nutty crunch, or served sweetened. Soak briefly, then use a toothpick to push out and remove the bitter green shoot from the center; finally, boil until tender.

Mung beans (dau xanh) These are the beans used to grow bean sprouts. Dried mung beans, or gram, range from green to yellow to black. Substitute slightly larger azuki, or even dried soybeans, black (turtle) beans or black-eyed peas (beans).

Mushrooms, dried black (nam huong kho) Dried black, or shiitake, mushrooms are actually dark gray to brown, available in varying grades from Asian shops. (Those with dark caps and deep ivory-colored creases are particularly valued.) The flavor is more pronounced than for fresh. Soak mushrooms in hot water for about 20 minutes, drain and remove tough stems. Strain soaking water to flavor stock.

Mushrooms, tree ear or cloud (black or white fungus) (moc nhi/nam tuyet) Available both fresh and dried. Trim the tough core before using. Dried fungus must be soaked and rinsed thoroughly. Textural, with little taste, it absorbs flavors during cooking. Also known as wood ear mushrooms.

Shallots (French shallots), brown and pink (hanh kho/hanh huong) Resembling clustered tiny onions, these bulbs may be pink to purple but, most commonly in Vietnam, they are brown to golden. They range in weight from 1/8 oz (4 g) to 1/4 oz (8g).

Mung beans (dau xanh)

Mushrooms, dried black (nam huong kho)

Mushrooms, tree ear or cloud (black or white fungus) (moc nhi/nam tuyet)

Shallots (French shallots), brown

Shallots (French shallots), pink

Sour fruits

Souring agents

Sugarcane (mia)

Tamarind (me)

Taro stem (bac ha/doc mung)

Sour fruits and souring agents (qua chua) Sour and astringent fruits, both cooked and raw, are widely used in Vietnam. These include underripe pineapple, green mango and green carambola (star fruit). Substitute tart apples, green plums, grapes or apricots. Pomello is preferred over bitter grapefruit. Both green papaya and green banana are deliciously astringent. Other souring agents include lemon and lime juice, tamarind and rice vinegar.

Sugarcane (mia) The stalk of the sugarcane plant is rich in sweet nectar, the basis of granulated white sugar, as well as a refreshing liquid beverage. A sharp machete and manual dexterity are both needed to hack sugarcane into usable pieces. Canned sugarcane pieces are available at Asian grocers.

Tamarind (me) The tart and sour pulp of one variety of tamarind pod. Do not confuse with sweet tamarind pods, which are candy-like and look almost identical. Easiest to use is commercial tamarind puree, available at many supermarkets. Thinner tamarind water is available at Indian and Middle Eastern grocers. To make it, soak dried tamarind pulp in boiling water, then strain. Because there can be a difference in sourness between commercial and homemade puree, the quantities required are variable.

Taro stem (bac ha/doc mung) Sometimes called "Vietnamese rhubarb" or "elephant ear," its taste is rather innocuous, but its crunch is delicious. Known in Japan as zuiki. European rhubarb is not similar. Peel before using. The most similar substitute is waterlily stems. **Caution:** Some varieties of taro are toxic. Purchase only from knowledgeable Asian grocers.

Basil, sweet Thai (rau hung que)
More fiery than Western basil and tasting less of aniseed or licorice. The most versatile of three Asian basil varieties, sweet Thai basil (bai horapa in Thai) is ubiquitous in Vietnamese cooking, and is always served with duck and dog.

Chives, Chinese (flat/garlic) (he)
Flat, dark green shoots, similar in length—but not width—to regular chives. The smell is akin to garlic. The bottom 1 inch (2.5 cm) or so is discarded. Flowering chives are also popular, but these round, woody stems are usually cooked like a vegetable, although tender shoots are served raw as an herb.

Cilantro (fresh coriander) (rau mui/rau ngo) The fresh leaves, stems and roots of the coriander plant. Not to be confused with coriander seed. Also known as Chinese parsley.

Dill (rau thi la) The fronds of fresh dill are a French introduction, but one embraced wholeheartedly, as in the famed fish dish Cha Ca (see page 88). Remove the tough central stem. Do not confuse with pickling dill, or fennel. Also known as "feather dill" or "baby dill."

Herbs (rau gia vi tuoi) Fresh herb sprigs, served at the table as a communal salad are essential to a Vietnamese meal (see Table Greens, page 50). These are some of the more popular offerings.

Basil, sweet Thai (rau hung que)

Chives, Chinese (flat/garlic) (he)

Cilantro (fresh coriander) (rau mui/rau ngo)

Dill (rau thi la)

Eryngo (sawtooth coriander) (rau mui tau/rau ngo gai) Similar in taste to cilantro, with long sawtooth-edged leaves. Especially delicious with fish and in sour tamarind dishes.

Fish leaf (fish mint) (rau diep ca) Heart-shaped leaves resembling ivy, tender with a sour undertone and a sharp and overwhelming fish taste. Eaten raw, fish leaf makes a surprising addition to beef salads and other grilled meat dishes.

Lemon balm, Vietnamese (rau kinh gioi) Vietnamese lemon balm is stronger than Western lemon balm, tasting both of mint and fragrant citrus. Substitute perilla or peppermint.

Mint (rau bac ha/rau huong lui) Fresh mint is essential to Vietnamese cooking. The sprightly oval- and mottle-leafed peppermint is particularly popular as a table green, while the more delicate arrow-shaped spearmint is less so.

Eryngo (sawtooth coriander) (rau mui tau/rau ngo gai)

Fish leaf (fish mint) (rau diep ca)

Lemon balm, Vietnamese (rau kinh gioi)

Mint (rau bac ha/rau huong lui)

Mint, Vietnamese (rau ram) The ubiquitous and slightly fiery polygonum is often—but not always—identified by a smudge-like blotch in the leaf's center, and its astringent mint tang. Its color ranges from green to purple. Occasionally called hot mint, laksa leaf or Vietnamese basil, it is actually not related to either mint or basil.

Perilla (shiso leaf) (rau tia to) Available in both red and green varieties, although the red type prevails in Vietnam. Perilla is the common shiso leaf of Japanese cookery, ranging in length from 1¼ inches (3 cm) to 4 inches (10 cm). It is related to both basil and mint, hence its wonderful adaptability.

Pennywort (rau ma) Because of its heavy-flowering top, this is sometimes called "crab claw herb." The small green oval leaves of this herb are slightly tart and the most prized. Pennywort also flavors a refreshingly cool drink.

Piper leaf (la lot) Shiny, dark green leaves about the size of ivy and innocuously mild. Add to stir-fries at the last minute. Use raw piper leaves to wrap individual portions of ground meat destined for charcoal grilling, or, conversely, to enfold bite-sized pieces of cooked meats. When unavailable, substitute blanched grape leaves. (See Glossary, page 123.)

Rice paddy herb (ngo om) Small green leaves with a cumin scent and sharp citrus taste.

Mint, Vietnamese (rau ram)

Perilla (shiso leaf) (rau tia to)

Pennywort (rau ma)

Piper leaf (la lot)

Rice paddy herb (ngo om)

Cellophane noodles (mien/bun tau)

Noodles Rice noodles, served at room temperature, readily take the place of steamed rice, especially at breakfast and lunch, when one-course meals are the norm. Use fresh noodles direct from the package, as they are already cooked and require no further preparation. Generally, the thicker sizes are used in soups.

Rice noodles (banh cuon)

Rice noodles (mi gao/banh/bun), Banh pho, Hu tieu

Rice paper sheets (banh da nem/banh trang)

Wheat or egg noodles (mi)

Cellophane noodles (mien/bun tau) Also known as bean thread vermicelli or glass noodles, these thin noodles are commonly made from mung bean starch or root starch. They are extremely tough, not brittle.

Rice noodles (mi gao/banh/bun) Dried, Available fresh in Vietnam, but dried overseas (see page 32 for preparation). Generally speaking, bun are round noodles while banh noodles are flat. **Banh cuon:** Fresh rice sheets made from a batter steamed directly on a stretched cloth. Served plain or rolled and stuffed. Variants also exist, with shrimp and chives cooked directly in the batter. **Banh hoi:** Angel-hair rice noodle sold dried in skeins swirled into square cakes. It often accompanies grilled meats. **Banh pho:** This rice noodle is preferred for pho, and is available fresh and dried in three widths. The thinnest is about $\frac{1}{16}$ inch (2 mm) wide. **Hu tieu:** Made from rice starch and blended with tapioca starch to make them more durable. Use in soups or in Chinese-style stir-fries. Available dried, and also called "rice sticks."

Rice paper sheets (banh da nem/banh trang) Very thin and brittle sheets made from ground rice amylose, and sometimes tapioca starch. Soften prior to using (see page 34), and eat raw, as in fresh spring rolls, or fried. Usually round, the two standard sizes are about 6 inches (15 cm) and 9 inches (23 cm) in diameter.

Wheat or egg noodles (mi) Thin to medium-wide egg and/or wheat noodles. Sold both fresh (refrigerated) and dried. Unlike rice noodles, they are not presoaked but are boiled until tender and drained before adding to some soups, such as steamboats, and to Chinese-style stir-fries.

Fresh rice noodles

1 Dried rice noodles

2

3

Step-by-step preparing rice noodles (bun)

While steamed rice is the focus of all Vietnamese evening meals, rice noodles are the favored partner for single-dish meals, particularly at breakfast and lunch. Use fresh noodles directly from the package, as they are already cooked and require no further preparation. Once refrigerated, they harden.

Dried rice noodles—especially thin vermicelli rice noodles—come in varying widths, from thin angel hair to thicker rice sticks. Generally speaking, thin noodles are softened and served at room temperature to accompany salads and grilled meats and are also used to fill fresh spring rolls. Thicker noodles are favored in soups and Chinese-style stir-fries.

Preparing dried rice noodles

1. Soak noodles in very hot water until just tender, 10–15 minutes, depending on thickness.

2. Drain and cover until ready to serve. Rice sticks require longer soaking, up to 30 minutes. Alternatively, plunge dried noodles into a large pot of gently boiling water. Stir to separate and cook until tender, 2–4 minutes. Drain and rinse immediately in cool water. Drain again.

3. Noodles for soup—both fresh and rehydrated—should be plunged for a moment into boiling water immediately prior to serving to reheat. Small, ladlelike baskets are traditional for this, and hold enough for one large single serving. Once heated, turn noodles directly into warmed individual soup bowls and add hot broth.

Step-by-step preparing cellophane noodles

Unlike rice noodles, cellophane (bean thread) noodles are commonly made from mung beans, as well as from the starchy root cu dong rieng. Interchangeable, these noodles are extremely tough and not brittle. They are a common ingredient in fried spring rolls and are also stir-fried on their own or simply tossed into a salad. Because they are extremely hard to cut, purchase them in small packages or bundles—no more than 3½ oz (100 g) each. They are always softened prior to using. In spite of their apparent resilience, prepare them at the last minute to preserve a springy texture.

1. Immerse in very hot, but not boiling, water for exactly 1 minute and drain. A subsequent cold-water bath stops the cooking process.

2. Use scissors to cut to desired length.

3. Cellophane noodles used directly from the packet can also be deep-fried until crisp and used as a garnish.

1

2

3

1

Step-by-step preparing rice paper sheets

As well as being used to make spring rolls, softened, round rice paper sheets are also served in piles at the table for wrapping foods to eat.

1. Place dry stacked rice paper sheets on a plate.

2. Cover with a damp cloth that has been wrung dry, and wrap tightly with plastic film for 1–2 hours to soften sheets slightly. Shuffle sheets occasionally for even moisture distribution. Alternatively, place 2–3 cabbage leaves alongside rice paper sheets on a flat plate, cover tightly with plastic wrap and leave overnight.

3. The sheets should peel away individually; take care not to tear them. If they are still brittle, lightly moisten by either brushing with water or wiping with a damp cloth. Do not over-moisten.

4. Large, 9-inch (23-cm) rice paper sheets for enfolding foods at the table are cut into thirds or halves, then stacked; use scissors or shears after softening. This makes them ideal for rolling bite-sized morsels. Precut sheets are sometimes available from Asian markets.

2

3

4

Quick treatment for spring rolls

This treatment is especially suited for sheets used for spring rolls, but less suited for sheets to be used for serving at the table.

1. Quickly dip each sheet, one at a time, into a pan of water (a shallow roasting pan works well).

1

2. Do not leave in water to soak, but pass sheet through water for a couple seconds, pat dry, then drain flat on a damp cloth. Do not over-moisten, as this leads to tearing, and sheets will not adhere easily when rolling. Be patient, as they will subsequently soften—taking from 15 seconds to a few minutes. Use immediately after they have softened, rolling into a spring roll.

2

3. If stacking, place sheets of waxed paper in between rice paper sheets, as the greater volume of water used in this method can oversoak sheets and make them unusable.

3

Ingredients

1

2

3

Step-by-step making fresh spring rolls

Soften a rice paper sheet following directions on page 35, then lay, smooth side down, on a damp cloth. In the illustrations we use a large rice paper sheet about 9 inches (23 cm) in diameter. Lay a lettuce leaf slightly off center along bottom of sheet. (Use a soft lettuce leaf, like butter (Boston) or oak leaf, with core removed.) Add herb leaves of your choice, first removing any stems that might pierce rice paper. Top with bean sprouts and softened dried or fresh thin rice noodles. The pile of fillings should be long and narrow, in the shape of a horizontal rectangle.

1. Fold over the two sides of rice paper sheet to enclose the two narrow ends of filling. Crease rice paper gently, then lay a few shoots of Chinese chives along top side of filling so that the ends stick out beyond edges of rice paper by about ½ inch (1.2 cm). Arrange 3 thin slices meat or halved shrimp on rice paper, about ¾ inch (2 cm) above chives, again horizontally along lines of filling. Meat should be cut very thin, about 1 x 1½ inches (2.5 x 4 cm) each, and medium shrimp should be sliced lengthwise and placed skin-side down.

2. Bring bottom of rice paper sheet up and over filling and press gently to compact. (At this point, you may need to lightly brush rice paper sheet with water along the two sides to facilitate rolling and sealing.) Continue rolling the filling into a fat cigar shape about 4 inches (10 cm) long and 1¼ inches (3 cm) wide, ensuring that filling is compact. Take care not to tear sheet.

3. Gently press rice paper sheet to seal it to itself.

Note: If sheets are too wet, they will not adhere. Decorative fillings, such as chives, shrimp and herb leaves, will be visible through rice paper. Keep covered with plastic wrap, while repeating steps to make remaining rolls.

Step-by-step making fried spring rolls

1. Soften a rice paper sheet following directions on page 35; here we use the smaller rice paper sheets, 6 inches (15 cm) in diameter. Wipe each rice paper sheet lightly with a damp cloth before using. If you like, add 1 teaspoon sugar to soaking water, as this will give it a crispier texture when fried. Cut off bottom and top thirds of a sheet to make 2 quarter moons. Lay one of these pieces at bottom edge of a full rice sheet to reinforce it. Reserve center sections for individually wrapping foods at the table, or trim corners with scissors to make more quarter-moon pieces.

2. Spoon a heaping tablespoon of filling across bottom middle of sheet, slightly off center. Press filling lightly into a cylindrical shape.

3. Fold bottom edge of rice paper sheet over filling, pressing gently to remove any air bubbles that might burst during cooking. Fold the two sides inward, creasing to reinforce fold, then proceed as in Step 3 on page 36. Lightly smear final fold at top with a paste of flour and water. The roll should be about ⅔ x 2 inches (1.75 x 5 cm) in size. Cover lightly with plastic wrap to prevent drying, and fill remaining rice paper sheets in the same way. (Do not add large fresh herbs and lettuce leaves to filling of fried spring rolls, as these wilt during cooking. Likewise, softened cellophane noodles are more common in fried spring rolls than the rice noodles used in fresh spring rolls.)

4. In a wok or deep fryer, heat 4 inches (10 cm) oil to 325–350°F (170–180°C) and fry spring rolls until crisp and golden brown, about 5 minutes (see Caution). Using a skimmer, transfer to paper towels to drain. Keep warm in a low oven while cooking successive batches.

To serve, wrap a spring roll in a crisp lettuce leaf, adding fresh herbs as desired (see Table Greens, page 50). Dip into Bean Sauce (page 114) or Nuoc Cham Sauce (page 116).

Caution: When deep-frying, make sure the wok or deep fryer is never filled more than one-third full, as the oil can froth up to double its volume when food is added, and any spilled oil can catch on fire.

Ingredients

12 medium shrimp (prawns), cooked, peeled and deveined

3½-oz (100-g) packet dried rice vermicelli noodles (bun)

12 leaves butter (Boston) lettuce

12 fresh leaves mint, preferably peppermint

12 Chinese (flat/garlic) chives, cut crosswise into thirds

12 sheets rice paper, about 9 inches (23 cm) in diameter

FOR ACCOMPANIMENTS

Bean Sauce (page 114)

Nuoc Cham Nem Sauce (page 116)

Fresh spring rolls with shrimp
Nem cuon song/Goi cuon

Remove tails from shrimp and cut shrimp in half lengthwise. Set aside.

Prepare dried noodles as described on page 32. Using scissors, cut noodles into manageable lengths.

Remove core from lettuce leaves. If using larger leaves, cut them so they are about 2 inches (5 cm) wide. Remove stems from mint, and prepare chives.

To make spring rolls, soften a rice paper sheet following directions on page 35, then assemble the rolls as described on page 36. Make sure to place shrimp halves, skin-side down, toward top of sheet, so they clearly show through final layer. Likewise, before final roll, arrange 2 or 3 chives lengthwise to poke out about ½ inch (1.2 cm) from each end.

Cover with plastic wrap to prevent rice paper from drying out. Rolls can be made up to 1–2 hours in advance. Serve with bean sauce or nuoc cham nem sauce.

Makes 12 rolls

Variations: With pork Substitute 12 very thin slices roasted pork loin for the shrimp, and proceed as above.

Vegetarian (Goi cuon dau hu) Omit shrimp. Add 8 oz (250 g) bean sprouts to filling, plus thinly sliced dried tofu (bean curd) skin, as desired.

Ingredients

6 dried black mushrooms

½ oz (15 g) dried, or 1 oz (30 g) fresh, tree ear or cloud mushrooms (black or white fungus)

1½-oz (50-g) packet cellophane (bean thread) noodles

1 turnip or kohlrabi, about 8 oz (250 g) peeled and grated

1 onion, shredded

1½ cups (3 oz/90 g) bean sprouts, rinsed and drained

1–2 scallions (shallots/green onions), including green parts, finely chopped

8 oz (250 g) lean ground pork, preferably shoulder

1 egg, beaten

¾ teaspoon ground pepper

about 45 sheets rice paper, about 9 inches (23 cm) diameter

1 teaspoon sugar dissolved in 1 cup (8 fl oz/250 ml) water (see page 37)

1 tablespoon flour dissolved in 2–3 teaspoons water (see page 37)

about 4–6 cups vegetable oil for deep-frying

FOR ACCOMPANIMENTS

Table Greens (page 50)

Nuoc Cham Nem Sauce (page 116)

Fried spring rolls
Nem ran Ha noi/Cha gio

Soak dried black mushrooms in hot water for about 20 minutes, then drain, squeezing to remove all liquid. Use scissors or a small knife to cut tough stems and discard. Cut mushroom caps into fine julienne and set aside. If using dried tree ear or cloud mushrooms, soak them separately in several changes of water to remove grit, then drain, squeezing to remove all water. Fresh tree ear or cloud mushrooms should be quickly rinsed, and patted dry; then remove tough whitish core and discard, and cut mushroom into thin strips.

Prepare dried noodles as described on page 33.

Pat shredded turnip and onion with a cloth to remove excess moisture. Cut bean sprouts into ½-inch (1.2-cm) lengths. Set vegetables and chopped scallions aside.

In a bowl, combine pork, vegetables, scallions and noodles. Add egg and toss to coat; season with pepper.

To make rolls, soften a rice paper sheet in the sugar water following directions on page 35. Add about 2–3 heaping tablespoons of filling, and roll (see page 37). Cover lightly with plastic wrap to prevent drying, and fill remaining wrappers in the same way.

In a wok or deep fryer, heat 4 inches (10 cm) oil to 325–350°F (170–180°C) and fry spring rolls, in batches, until crisp and golden brown, about 6 minutes (see Caution). Using a skimmer, transfer to paper towels to drain. Keep warm in a low oven while cooking successive batches. To serve, wrap each roll in a piece of lettuce, plus herbs of choice, and dip in nuoc cham nem sauce, spooning some vegetables from sauce into lettuce roll.

Makes 30 rolls

Note: In southern Vietnam, fried spring rolls are made with the smaller (6-inch/15-cm) rice paper sheets and are called cha gio. The northern nem is larger, about the size of a cigar.

Caution: When deep-frying, make sure the wok or deep fryer is never filled more than one-third full, as the oil can froth up to double its volume when food is added, and any spilled oil can catch on fire. Fried spring rolls are cooked in oil at relatively low temperatures. High heat may cause the rolls to burst while frying.

Variation: With rice noodles Rice vermicelli noodles (bun) (see page 32) can substitute for the cellophane noodles. Alternatively, use cold cooked rice.

Fried crab nems
Nem cua be/Cha gio cua be

If using dried tree ear or cloud mushrooms, soak them separately in several changes of water to remove grit, then drain, squeezing to remove all water. Fresh tree ear mushrooms should be quickly rinsed, and patted dry; then remove tough whitish core and discard, and cut mushroom into thin strips.

Pat shredded carrot and onion with a cloth to remove excess moisture. Cut bean sprouts into ½-inch (1.2-cm) lengths. Cut scallions into thin rounds.

Prepare dried noodles as described on page 32. Using scissors, cut noodles into manageable lengths.

Squeeze crabmeat firmly in your hand to extract any moisture. In a bowl, combine crabmeat, vegetables and noodles. Add egg and toss to coat; season with pepper.

To make rolls, soften a rice paper sheet in the sugar water following directions on page 35. Add about 2–3 heaping tablespoons of filling, and roll (see page 37). Cover lightly with plastic wrap to prevent drying, and fill remaining wrappers in the same way.

In a wok or deep fryer, heat 4 inches (10 cm) oil to 325–350°F (170–180°C) and fry spring rolls in batches, until crisp and golden brown, about 5 minutes (see Caution). Transfer to paper towels to drain. Keep warm in a low oven while cooking successive batches.

Serve with nuoc cham nem sauce and table greens.

Makes 30 rolls

Caution: When deep-frying, make sure the wok or deep fryer is never filled more than one-third full, as the oil can froth up to double its volume when food is added, and any spilled oil can catch on fire. Fried crab nems are cooked in oil at relatively low temperatures. High heat may cause the rolls to burst while frying.

Ingredients

½ oz (15 g) dried, or 1 oz (30 g) fresh, tree ear or cloud mushrooms (black or white fungus)

1 carrot, peeled and shredded

1 small onion, shredded

1 cup (2 oz/60 g) bean sprouts, rinsed and drained

3 scallions (shallots/spring onions), including green parts

1½-oz (45-g) packet dried rice vermicelli noodles (bun)

8 oz (250 g) cooked or lump crabmeat, picked over for shell

1 egg, beaten

ground pepper to taste

1 teaspoon sugar dissolved in 1 cup (8 fl oz/250 ml) water (see page 37)

1 tablespoon flour dissolved in 2–3 teaspoons water (see page 37)

about 45 sheets rice paper, about 9 inches (23 cm) in diameter

about 4–6 cups vegetable oil for deep-frying

FOR ACCOMPANIMENTS

Nuoc Cham Nem Sauce (page 116)

Table Greens (page 50)

Ingredients

12-inch (30-cm) piece of fresh sugarcane or one 12-oz (375-g) can sugarcane packed in light syrup, drained

1 lb (500 g) shelled raw shrimp (green prawns), deveined

1 teaspoon fish sauce

2 tablespoons finely ground fresh pork fatback (optional)

6 cloves garlic, finely chopped

2 tablespoons finely chopped brown or pink shallots (French shallots)

½ teaspoon ground pepper

2 teaspoons sugar

1 egg white

1 tablespoon fish sauce

1–2 tablespoons ground rice (see Hint)

FOR ACCOMPANIMENTS

Bean Sauce (page 114)

Nuoc Cham Nem Sauce (page 116)

Sugarcane shrimp
Tom bao mia/Chao tom

Use a cleaver to peel sugarcane, then hack it crosswise into 4-inch (10-cm) pieces. Split each piece lengthwise into quarters. Canned sugarcane is usually thinner, and should be cut in half lengthwise. It is much easier to use. You should have a total of 12 pieces.

In a bowl, toss shrimp with 1 teaspoon fish sauce. Let stand for 15 minutes. Wipe thoroughly with paper towels, then squeeze any excess moisture from shrimp. Transfer to a food processor and chop finely. Add pork fatback if using, garlic, shallots, pepper and sugar and process to a sticky paste, scraping the sides of the container as necessary. Add egg white, 1 tablespoon fish sauce and ground rice, and process again. Chill slightly to facilitate molding into small balls; although this step is optional.

Lightly moisten your hands with oil and shape about 2 tablespoons paste into a mound around each piece of sugarcane. Leave about 1 inch (2.5 cm) sugarcane exposed at each end.

Prepare a charcoal grill (barbecue) or brazier following directions on page 18, or preheat an oven broiler (grill) with the grilling rack set about 5 inches (12 cm) from heat source. Cook, turning occasionally, until dark golden on all sides, 3–5 minutes. Watch carefully, as it tends to char quickly. Alternatively, preheat oven to 350°F (180°C/Gas 4) and bake, turning occasionally, for about 30 minutes. Serve with bean sauce or nuoc cham nem sauce.

Makes 12

Hint: To make ground rice In a wok or small frying pan over low–medium heat, stir 2–3 tablespoons sticky (glutinous) rice until golden-brown, 3–5 minutes. Transfer to a mortar and pound to a coarse powder with a pestle.

Do not confuse the ground rice called for in this recipe with rice starch, which is sometimes labeled "flour."

Variation: In rice paper rolls Although these are delicious served simply with a sauce dip, it is usual in Vietnam for the shrimp to be removed from the sugarcane after cooking and wrapped in lettuce leaves along with thinly sliced cucumber, fresh herbs of choice, rice vermicelli (bun) and chopped roasted peanuts. Roll in a softened rice paper sheet and dip into desired sauce.

Ingredients

4 oz (125 g) fresh pork fatback, ground or finely diced

1 lb (500 g) ground beef, preferably sirloin (rump) (see Note)

¼ cup (¾ oz/20 g) finely chopped brown or pink shallots (French shallots)

3 large cloves garlic, finely chopped

1 fresh small red chili, seeded and finely chopped

2 tablespoons fish sauce

1 tablespoon sugar

1 teaspoon salt

1 teaspoon ground pepper

juice of 1 lemon

about 60 piper leaves or grape leaves (see Hint)

FOR ACCOMPANIMENTS

Table Greens (page 50)

rice paper sheets, softened (see page 34), and cut into halves or thirds

Nuoc Cham Nem Sauce (page 116)

Grilled beef wrapped in leaves
Bo nuong la lot

In a bowl, combine all ingredients except piper leaves. Use your hands to knead well, for about 3 minutes. Meanwhile, soak 60 wooden toothpicks in water for a few minutes to prevent charring.

Place a piper leaf, dark side down, on a work surface. Place about 1 tablespoon filling in middle of leaf and roll into a tiny cylinder about 2 inches (5 cm) long and ¾ inch (2 cm) thick. Make sure that meat is fully covered by the leaf, although covering the two ends is optional. Skewer with a toothpick. Continue with remaining meat and leaves. Alternatively, form meat into small patties and thread several patties onto two skewers, leaving enough space between them to cook all sides fully.

Prepare a charcoal grill (barbecue) or brazier following directions on page 18, or preheat an oven broiler (grill) with the grilling rack set about 5 inches (12 cm) from heat source. Cook parcels, turning twice, until cooked through, about 8–10 minutes. Watch carefully, as they tend to char quickly.

Serve with table greens, tearing lettuce to enfold the cooked parcel and adding other fresh herbs to taste, and rice papers for wrapping. Dip into nuoc cham nem sauce, spooning some of the vegetables onto the roll.

Makes about 60

Note: If ground sirloin is unavailable, use regular ground (minced) stewing steak (chuck or hamburger), as it has more flavor than lean ground round (topside). The fat content in ground beef produces a more tender product, as the melting fat bastes the patties internally during cooking.

Hint: If piper leaves are unavailable, use cured grape leaves. Alternatively, use aluminum foil.

Ingredients

6 dried black mushrooms

1 bunch Chinese (flat/garlic) chives, trimmed

6 eggs

vegetable oil for cooking

1¼ lb (625 g) finely ground lean pork

1 teaspoon ground pepper

3 tablespoons fish sauce

Pork omelet roll
Trung hap van

Soak mushrooms in hot water for about 20 minutes, then drain, squeezing to remove all liquid. Use scissors or a small knife to cut away and discard tough stems. Cut mushroom caps into thin julienne and set aside. Cut chives into 8-inch (20-cm) lengths.

Prepare 6 thin, flat omelets, as described on page 121.

In a food processor, combine ground pork, pepper and fish sauce and process until well blended, about 1 minute. Alternatively, use your hands to knead well, about 3 minutes. The smoother the paste, the better. Divide meat into 6 portions.

Lay out an omelet and spread one meat portion evenly on it. Lay strips of mushroom and chive shoots evenly across the entire top, arranging them horizontally to facilitate rolling. Tightly roll omelet into a cylinder. Wrap tightly with plastic wrap, twisting the ends to secure. Repeat with remaining omelets. Place wrapped rolls in a steamer over—but not touching—rapidly boiling water. Cover tightly with a lid and steam for about 20 minutes, or until the meat is thoroughly cooked.

Use tongs to remove the rolls from steamer. Let the rolls cool, then remove plastic wrap and cut the rolls into rounds about ¼ inch (6 mm) thick. Arrange these on a platter, such as in the fan-shape of a peacock's tail. These rolls are traditionally served plain. If desired, accompany with lettuce leaves, softened rice vermicelli (bun) (see page 32) and Nuoc Cham Sauce (page 116). Tear a piece of lettuce to enfold the roll with some noodles and fresh herbs of choice, and dip into sauce.

Makes 6 rolls

Silky pork sausage

Gio lua/Cha lua

In a food processor or meat grinder, grind pork until it is extremely smooth. Add all remaining ingredients except banana leaf, and process well. Turn out into a bowl and work with your hands for a few minutes until meat becomes slightly gluey.

Wipe banana leaf with a clean cloth before using. Tear or cut banana leaf into a 12-inch (30-cm) square, removing its hard center stem. The tip portion of leaf is best to use. Soften leaf by running it briefly over a gas flame until the milky or waxy side becomes shiny. Alternatively, substitute a square of heavy-duty aluminum foil. Lightly moisten your hands and mound the ground pork in center of leaf, then form it into a large sausage about 5 inches (12 cm) in diameter. Bring the 2 long sides together, then fold ends down and inward as if wrapping a boxed gift. Wrap tightly with plastic wrap and secure firmly.

Place the roll in a pot of gently boiling water and place an inverted plate on top of the roll to keep it submerged. Lower the heat to a bare simmer and cook, uncovered, until an instant-read thermometer inserted into the roll registers 140°F (60°C) for safety to a maximum 165–170°F (75°C), about 1 hour. (Add more boiling water as necessary during cooking.) Remove from water and let cool.

To serve, remove banana leaf, cut into slices ⅓ inch (1 cm) thick and accompany with sweet pickles, fresh long red chili slices, rice and nuoc cham sauce. The cooked roll can be refrigerated for up to 1 week.

Makes 1 large loaf

Note: This is a very versatile sausage that can be served simply with rice and fish sauce, or thinly sliced in a baguette sandwich, or used in various dishes such as fried rice or Seaweed Salad (page 61). It is available ready-made at any Vietnamese market.

Ingredients

1 lb (500 g) pork loin, trimmed and cut into 1-inch (2.5-cm) chunks

2 tablespoons tapioca starch or arrowroot

1 teaspoon baking soda

1 tablespoon fish sauce

½ teaspoon ground black pepper

1 large banana leaf

FOR ACCOMPANIMENTS

sweet Vietnamese pickles, such as pickled leeks (cu kieu), optional

fresh long red chilies, seeded and thinly sliced

Steamed Rice (page 120)

Nuoc Cham Sauce (page 116)

Ingredients

fresh herbs of choice, such as sprigs of cilantro (fresh coriander) (rau mui/rau ngo), peppermint and spearmint (rau baa ha/rau huong lui), Vietnamese mint (rau ram), perilla (rau tia to), Vietnamese lemon balm (rau kinh gioi), eryngo (sawtooth coriander) (rau mui tau/rau ngo gai), piper leaf (bo la lot), and sweet Thai basil (rau hung que); see Ingredients pages 28-30

leaves from 1–2 heads butter (Boston) lettuce

leaves from 1 red or green leaf lettuce (oak leaf, Lollo Rossa or coral)

2 cups (4 oz/125 g) bean sprouts, rinsed and drained

½ cucumber, seeded and thinly sliced

Table greens
Rau song/Rau thom

Trim herb stems and rinse leaves. Keep sprigs whole. Clean lettuce leaves. Rinse sprouts, and remove "tails" if desired. Prepare cucumber.

To serve, arrange lettuce leaves and herbs to one side of a large bowl or platter, and place sprouts and cucumber on the other side.

Serves 4–6

Note: This is a typical salad to accompany any Vietnamese meal. Vary your use of lettuce and herbs as desired. You can also, to a lesser extent, use pennywort (rau ma), the miniature, cumin-scented rice paddy herb (ngo om) and strong-tasting fish leaf (rau diep ca). Unlike a Western salad, where each diner has their own bowl, the greens are picked from a central platter. Lettuce leaves are torn to a suitable size to wrap bite-sized pieces of meat. Softened sheets of rice paper (see page 34) often accompany this salad.

Hint: Lettuce may be cleaned and refrigerated prior to use; this helps to crisp the leaves. Herbs can be delicate so they should be kept dry and refrigerated in plastic bags. Only rinse immediately prior to serving.

Variation: Soup herbs (Thom mui) A smaller selection of fresh herbs, specifically accompanying various soup dishes and some starter courses, includes scallions (shallots/spring onions), eryngo (sawtooth coriander) leaves, cilantro (fresh coriander) sprigs, Vietnamese mint (rau ram), dill and bean sprouts. Accompany with fresh long red chilies cut into small rings, fish sauce or Nuoc Cham Sauce (page 116), and lemon or lime wedges.

Chicken salad with herbs

Nom ga xe

To make pickled onions: Plunge pearl onions into boiling water, then drain and slip off the skins. If using pickling onions, peel and quarter. In a medium bowl, combine vinegar, sugar and fish sauce. Add onion and let stand for 10–15 minutes.

If using raw chicken, bring water or stock to a boil in a medium saucepan and add chicken. Immediately reduce heat to a low simmer and cook chicken until opaque throughout, 5–7 minutes. Transfer to a plate and let cool. Shred with your fingers or 2 forks into coarse long shreds. Set aside.

Plunge sprouts in a pot of boiling water, then drain immediately and refresh in cold water. Roll several Vietnamese mint leaves at a time into a tight bundle and cut into thin crosswise slices. Repeat to shred all leaves.

At the last moment, in a bowl, toss together onions and their marinade, chicken, bean sprouts, Vietnamese mint and chilies. Season with lime juice, salt and pepper. If desired, garnish with chilies.

Serves 6

Note: This dish is popular throughout Vietnam, although it originates in the south. Fiery Vietnamese mint gives the salad a fresh, floral quality.

Hint: Jars of prepared sweet pickled leeks (cu kieu) are available in Vietnamese and some Asian markets. These are time-saving; use in place of pickled onions in this recipe.

Ingredients

FOR PICKLED ONIONS

1 tablespoon rice vinegar or distilled white vinegar

1 teaspoon sugar

2 tablespoons fish sauce

1 lb (500 g) pearl onions or small boiling onions (pickling onions)

1 lb (500 g) boneless, skinless chicken thighs and/or breasts, or about 3 cups (18 oz/550 g) coarsely shredded cooked chicken, bones and skin removed

about 3 cups (24 fl oz/750 ml) water or stock for cooking chicken, if required

2 cups (4 oz/125 g) bean sprouts, rinsed and drained

leaves from ½ bunch Vietnamese mint (rau ram)

3 fresh long red chilies, seeded and coarsely chopped

juice of 3 limes, freshly squeezed

1 teaspoon salt

½ teaspoon ground pepper

chilies for garnish (optional)

Ingredients

1 fresh banana flower or 2 x 20 oz (750g) cans or bottles of banana blossom

juice of 1 lemon, plus 3–4 tablespoons fresh lemon juice or to taste

1 tablespoon salt, plus 1 teaspoon

2 boneless, skinless chicken breast halves (about 6 oz/185 g each) or 2 cups (10 oz/300 g) diced cooked chicken, firmly packed

about 2 cups (16 fl oz/500 ml) water or stock for cooking chicken, if required

vegetable oil for cooking

6 oz (180 g) pork fillet

1 carambola (star fruit), cut into thin stars

3 tablespoons sugar, plus more to taste if needed

1/2 cup (1 1/2 oz/45 g) small dried shrimp (optional)

2 tablespoons rice vinegar or distilled white vinegar (optional)

2 eggs

2 fresh long red chilies, seeded and thinly sliced

1 1/2 cups (3 oz/90 g) bean sprouts, rinsed and drained

1/3 cup (1/2 oz/15 g) coarsely torn Vietnamese mint (rau ram) sprigs

1/3 cup (1/2 oz/15 g) coarsely torn cilantro (fresh coriander) sprigs

1/3 cup (2 oz/60 g) peanuts, lightly toasted (see Hint, page 55) and lightly crushed or chopped

1/3 cup (2 oz/60 g) sesame seeds, lightly toasted (see Hint, page 55)

Banana flower **salad**

Nom hoa chuoi

Pull off outer 4–6 petals or bracts of fresh banana flower, and reserve. Pull remaining bracts from flower's core, discarding sticky white banana "shoots" inside each layer, as these are bitter. If using canned banana blossom, rinse and drain. Slice banana flower very thinly crosswise. Fill a medium bowl half full with water and add juice of 1 lemon and 1 tablespoon salt. Place flower slices in lemon water and let stand for 1 hour to soften; drain and pat dry.

If using raw chicken, bring water or stock to a simmer in a large saucepan and poach chicken until barely opaque throughout, about 5 minutes. In a frying pan over medium heat, heat a small amount of vegetable oil. Add pork and fry on both sides until cooked through, about 5 minutes. Shred or thinly slice both meats; let cool.

Sprinkle carambola slices with 1 tablespoon of sugar and set aside. If using dried shrimp, simmer in water seasoned with vinegar and a pinch of sugar until softened, about 10 minutes.

Prepare 2 thin omelets as described on page 121. Cut omelets into thin strips and set aside.

In a bowl, combine banana flower, chicken, pork, shrimp, carambola, chilies and bean sprouts. Add 3 tablespoons lemon juice, 1 teaspoon salt and remaining 2 tablespoons sugar. Taste, and adjust seasoning with lemon juice if necessary. Toss in half of herbs. Spoon mixture into reserved banana petals and top each serving with omelet strips, peanuts, sesame seeds and remaining herbs.

Serves 4–6

Note: Canned banana blossom is available at most Asian markets. If unavailable, double quantity of bean sprouts for bulk.

Hint: To lightly toast peanuts and sesame seeds Heat a dry wok or frying pan over medium heat, add peanuts or sesame seeds and toast, stirring constantly, until lightly golden and fragrant. Alternatively, preheat oven to 400°F (200°C/Gas 6). Spread peanuts or sesame seeds on a baking sheet and toast, shaking once or twice to ensure even browning, until lightly golden and fragrant, 8–12 minutes for peanuts and 8–10 minutes for sesame seeds. Immediately remove from oven, lest they become bitter.

Green papaya salad **with beef**

Nom bo kho

Grate papaya and carrots into thin long strips. Toss together, cover, and refrigerate until ready to serve.

Cut beef into thin, wide pieces. In a medium bowl, stir all marinade ingredients together. Add beef and toss to coat. Refrigerate for 2 hours, stirring occasionally.

To make dressing: Place garlic cloves in a mortar, and using pestle crush to a paste. In a medium bowl, combine with remaining dressing ingredients.

Prepare a charcoal grill (barbecue) or brazier following directions on page 18. Alternatively, preheat an oven broiler (grill). Cook beef, arranged in a single layer, turning once, until lightly browned, about 2 minutes on each side. You may need to cook beef in 2 or 3 batches.

In a wok or deep fryer, heat 1 cup (8 fl oz/250 ml) oil. Add meat, a few pieces at a time, and fry until slightly crisp, 1–2 minutes. Take care that the oil does not sputter or boil over. Using a slotted spoon, transfer to paper towels to drain. Use kitchen shears or scissors to cut meat into matchsticks, and set aside.

Immediately before serving, add shredded vegetables to dressing and toss to coat. Arrange papaya and carrot on a large, deep platter. Top with meat and sprinkle with peanuts and herbs.

Serves 6

Note: If unripe papaya is not available, increase quantity of carrot, or use peeled, shredded cucumber.

Ingredients

½ green papaya (about 1 lb/500 g), peeled and seeded

1 carrot, peeled

12 oz (375 g) sirloin or rump steak, trimmed

1 cup (8 fl oz/250 ml) vegetable oil for deep-frying

1 cup (6 oz/185 g) peanuts, lightly toasted (see Hint page 55) and coarsely chopped

FOR MARINADE

1 tablespoon fish sauce

large pinch sugar

2 cloves garlic, coarsely chopped

1 tablespoon coarsely chopped brown or pink shallots (French shallots)

1 teaspoon chili powder

¼ teaspoon five-spice powder

1 teaspoon ground pepper

⅓ cup (½ oz/15 g) chopped Vietnamese lemon balm

⅓ cup (½ oz/15 g) coarsely torn cilantro (fresh coriander) sprigs

FOR DRESSING

⅓ cup (3 fl oz/90 ml) fish sauce

¼ cup (2 fl oz/60 ml) rice vinegar or distilled white vinegar

2 teaspoons sugar

9 cloves garlic

½ teaspoon ground pepper

½ teaspoon salt

Ingredients

FOR MARINATED VEGETABLES

1 cucumber

4 carrots

2 stalks celery, chopped fine julienne

6 oz (185 g) pearl onions or small boiling onions (pickling onions)

1 tablespoon rice vinegar or distilled white vinegar

1 teaspoon sugar

1 tablespoon fish sauce

2 teaspoons salt

1 fresh long red chili seeded and chopped

1½ cups (3 oz/90 g) bean sprouts, rinsed and drained

FOR LOBSTER

1 lb (500 g) shelled meat from lobster tails or langoustines (scampi/saltwater crayfish)

1 tablespoon fish sauce

¼ teaspoon ground pepper

½ teaspoon chili powder or to taste

2 teaspoons finely chopped brown or pink shallots (French shallots)

½-inch (1.2-cm) knob fresh ginger, peeled and finely grated

FOR DRESSING

1 teaspoon Asian (toasted) sesame oil

2 teaspoons water

1 tablespoon fresh lime juice

½ teaspoon grated fresh ginger or ginger juice

¼ fresh long red chili, seeded and finely chopped

½ teaspoon salt

¼ teaspoon ground pepper

2 tablespoons coarsely chopped cilantro (fresh coriander) sprigs for garnish

Lobster salad
Xa lat tom hum

To make marinated vegetables: Cut cucumber lengthwise in half, then use a spoon to scoop out and discard seeds. Cut carrots and cucumber into strips the size of French fries. Plunge pearl onions into boiling water, then drain and slip off the skins. If using pickling onions, peel and quarter. In a medium bowl, combine vinegar, sugar, fish sauce, salt and chili. Add vegetables and sprouts and toss to coat. Let stand for 15–20 minutes.

Cut lobster meat into medallions about ½ inch (1.2 cm) thick. In a medium bowl, combine fish sauce, pepper, chili powder, shallots and ginger. Add lobster and toss to coat. Let stand for 10 minutes. In a large nonstick frying pan over medium-high heat, sauté lobster until opaque, about 2 minutes.

In a small bowl, combine all dressing ingredients. Add to lobster and toss to coat.

To serve, drain marinated vegetables and arrange on a serving plate. Layer lobster medallions on top and sprinkle with cilantro.

Serves 6–8

Seaweed salad

Nom rau cau

Prepare silky pork sausage as directed on page 49. Cut into julienne and set aside.

Soak seaweed in several changes of water in a very large bowl for 1 hour, then rinse well to remove grit or slime; drain. Use scissors to cut into manageable lengths.

Prepare omelets as described on page 121. Roll omelets, cut into strips and set aside.

In a large pot, bring about 3 quarts (3 L) water to a boil. Add crushed ginger and soaked seaweed, and cook for 1 minute. Drain immediately by pouring into a colander, discarding the ginger. Let seaweed cool, and pat dry.

In a salad bowl, toss seaweed, chicken and pork sausage together. In a small bowl, combine fish sauce, lemon or lime juice and sugar; stir until dissolved then add chilies and pepper. Add to seaweed mixture and toss through. To serve, sprinkle with omelet strips, peanuts and sesame seeds, and serve with table greens.

Serves 6–8

Note: This is a classic Hanoi recipe, still widely eaten in the non-touristy restaurants of the capital's Old Quarter.

Hints: For convenience, you can replace silky pork sausage with cooked pork sausage such as mortadella or frankfurter.

Vietnamese dried seaweed (rau cau) is straggly yet fine and tan to gray in color. It is available at Asian grocers and in some natural foods stores (see Ingredients, page 21). Other Asian dried seaweed may be substituted.

Ingredients

5 oz (150 g) Silky Pork Sausage (page 49) (see also Hints)

4-oz (125-g) packet Vietnamese dried seaweed (rau cau) (see Hints)

3 eggs

vegetable oil for cooking

1-inch (2.5-cm) knob fresh ginger, crushed

about 2 cups loosely packed (10 oz/300 g) shredded or coarsely chopped cooked chicken

½ cup (4 fl oz/125 ml) fish sauce

juice of 3 lemons or limes

2 tablespoons sugar or to taste

2–3 fresh long red chilies, seeded and cut into thin strips

2 teaspoons ground pepper

TO SERVE

3 tablespoons peanuts, lightly toasted (see Hint, page 55) and coarsely crushed

3 tablespoons sesame seeds, lightly toasted (see Hint, page 55)

Table Greens (page 50)

Ingredients

2 taro stems (Vietnamese rhubarb) (bac ha/doc mung), about 7 oz (220 g) (optional)

2 carambolas (star fruits), preferably slightly unripe

1 pineapple, preferably slightly unripe

2–3 tablespoons vegetable oil

2 small tomatoes, preferably slightly unripe, quartered

2 tablespoons fish sauce

2 tablespoons lemon juice

½ teaspoon ground pepper

2–3 tablespoons tamarind puree (to taste)

1–2 teaspoons sugar (to taste)

2 cups (8 fl oz/250 ml) water, or weak stock (see page 118)

4 oz (125 g) okra, thinly sliced

1 large leek or 3 baby leeks (white part only), well rinsed and thinly sliced, or 3 scallions (shallots/spring onions), including green parts, thinly sliced

2 lb (1 kg) shelled jumbo shrimp (king prawns), deveined

5 fresh eryngo (sawtooth coriander) leaves, very coarsely chopped, or ⅓ cup (½ oz/15 g) coarsely chopped cilantro (fresh coriander) sprigs

1 fresh long red chili, seeded and thinly sliced

FOR ACCOMPANIMENTS

Steamed Rice (page 120)

Soup Herbs (see Variation, page 50), including dill and eryngo (sawtooth coriander) leaves

2 lemons or limes, cut into wedges

SOUPS

Sour shrimp soup
Canh tom chua

If using taro, peel stem by pulling upward at base. The stem should come away easily in ribbon-like strips; do not use a vegetable peeler. Cut taro stem into small chunks and set aside. Cut carambola into thick stars about ¼ inch (6 mm) thick. Peel pineapple, core and cut into large chunks (see Note).

In a large pot, heat oil over medium-high heat. Add half of the tomatoes and cook just until they become watery, about 3 minutes. Add fish sauce, pineapple, carambola and lemon juice. Add pepper, 2 tablespoons of tamarind, and sugar to taste. Add water or stock, then okra, taro (if using), leek and remaining uncooked tomatoes. Taste and add remaining 1 tablespoon tamarind for a more sour taste, if desired. Bring to a rolling boil for 2 minutes, meanwhile adding shrimp to cook: raw shrimp until pink, 1–2 minutes, or cooked shrimp until hot, about 30 seconds. Remove pot promptly from heat, stir in eryngo leaves and chili slices. Serve piping hot with steamed rice and accompany with soup herbs and wedges of lemon or lime.

Serves 6–8

Note: Tinned pineapple may be substituted for fresh pineapple. If using tinned pineapple, reduce amount of sugar added to soup.

Hint: Frozen shrimp should be thawed in the refrigerator prior to using. Thawing at room temperature results in greater water loss and tougher shrimp.

Variation: With fish (Canh ca chua/Canh ca loc) Substitute shrimp with an equal quantity of fish fillets with skin on. Cut fish into large 2-inch (5-cm) pieces and cook until opaque throughout, 2–3 minutes. Traditionally, this is made with a freshwater fish known in Vietnam as loc, but good substitutes include thin fillets of trout or redfish.

Tart fish **soup** **with turmeric**

Canh ca chua

Using a pestle, pound turmeric in a mortar, or alternatively use a grater. Soak extracted juice and pulp in 1 tablespoon water, from 3–4 minutes up to a few hours; then strain. Wear gloves to prevent turmeric staining your skin.

In a small bowl, combine strained turmeric or turmeric powder, 3 tablespoons of fish sauce and pepper. Coat fish pieces with sauce mixture and let stand at room temperature for 20 minutes.

In a medium pot, heat oil over medium heat. Add leek and stir, cover, and cook for 2 minutes. Add tomatoes, remaining 1 tablespoon fish sauce and water, and stir. Cover and reduce heat to low. Cook until tomatoes are just soft, about 5 minutes. Add stock and bring to a boil. Add carambola, fish and its marinade, and half of chilies. Cook, increasing heat to high, until fish is opaque throughout, about 3 minutes for fillets and 5 minutes for steaks. Add bean sprouts, chives and herbs. Just before serving, garnish with remaining chili. Serve hot with steamed rice and an accompanying plate of soup herbs. Season to taste with fish sauce or nuoc cham sauce.

Serves 4–6

Note: The Vietnamese word "canh" describes a thin vegetable stock, with or without meat/seafood, that is usually served accompanying steamed rice.

Ingredients

- ¾-inch (2-cm) knob fresh turmeric, or 2 teaspoons ground turmeric
- 4 tablespoons (2 fl oz/60 ml) fish sauce
- 1 teaspoon ground pepper
- 2 lb (1 kg) catfish, cut through the bone into ¾-inch (2-cm) steaks (cutlets), or about 20 oz (600 g) fish fillets
- 3 tablespoons vegetable oil
- 1 large leek or 3 baby leeks, white part only, well rinsed and thinly sliced, or 3 scallions (shallots/spring onions), including green parts, thinly sliced
- 2 small tomatoes, cut into wedges
- 1 tablespoon water
- 4 cups (32 fl oz/1 L) Chicken Stock (page 118), Fish Stock (page 118) or diluted canned chicken broth
- 1–2 carambolas (star fruits), preferably slightly unripe, coarsely cut
- 1 fresh long red chili, seeded and thinly sliced lengthwise
- 2 cups (4 oz/125 g) bean sprouts, rinsed and drained
- ½ bunch Chinese (flat/garlic) chives
- ⅓ cup (½ oz/15 g) very coarsely chopped eryngo (sawtooth coriander) leaves or 1 cup (1⅓ oz/40 g) coarsely chopped cilantro (fresh coriander) sprigs
- ⅓ cup (½ oz/15 g) very coarsely chopped fresh dill

FOR ACCOMPANIMENTS

Steamed Rice (page 120)

Soup Herbs (see Variation, page 50)

fish sauce or Nuoc Cham Sauce (page 116)

Ingredients

3 lb (1.5 kg) raw or cooked crab in its shell, or 1½ lb (24 oz/750 g) lump crabmeat, picked over for shell

6 cups (48 fl oz/1.5 L) water, or if using precooked crab Quick Seafood Stock (page 118) or Fish Stock (page 118)

3 tablespoons vegetable oil

1 cup (4 oz/125 g) thinly sliced pink or brown shallots (French shallots)

¼ cup (2 fl oz/60 ml) Asian chili sauce (see Ingredients, page 20)

12-oz (375-g) packet dried rice noodles

1 bunch spinach (English spinach), stemmed and rinsed well

2 tablespoons fish sauce, plus more for serving

1–2 teaspoons salt (to taste)

freshly ground pepper to taste

1–2 lemons, quartered

Spicy crab and rice noodle **soup**

Canh banh da cua

If using raw crabs, scrub them with a scouring brush under cold running water, then plunge them into a deep pot of lightly salted boiling water—about 6 cups (48 fl oz/1.5 L). Cook for 10–15 minutes, depending on size. Remove crabs with a slotted spoon, reserving cooking liquid. Clean crabs by pulling off apron flap from under shell. Pry off top shell and rinse away breathing ducts or lungs. Break or cut body in half, or cut large crabs into smaller pieces. Twist off claws, reserving pincers for garnish. Refrigerate until ready to use.

In a small saucepan, heat oil over medium heat and sauté one-quarter of shallots with the chili sauce until shallots are soft, 3–5 minutes; set aside.

Prepare dried noodles as described on page 32.

Bring 6 cups reserved cooking liquid from crab, (or stock if using precooked crab), to a rapid boil. Add remaining ¾ cup shallots, spinach, crab and 2 tablespoons fish sauce. Stir to combine, and taste, adding salt if necessary. Remove from heat to avoid overcooking the crab.

Immediately prior to serving, reheat noodles by plunging them into boiling water for a moment, then drain. Divide among warmed large, deep soup bowls. Ladle hot soup over noodles, sprinkle with pepper, and add a dollop of reserved cooked chili sauce to each. (This dish is traditionally served very spicy.) Serve piping hot, with additional fish sauce to taste and lemon quarters on the side.

Serves 6

Note: This dish is a morning-market specialty of Hue.

Crab and asparagus **soup**

Sup cua mang xanh Da Lat

If using raw crabs, scrub them with a scouring brush under cold running water, then plunge them into a deep pot of lightly salted boiling water—about 6 cups (48 fl oz/1.5 L). Cook for 10–15 minutes, depending on size. Remove crabs with a slotted spoon, reserving cooking liquid. Clean crabs by pulling off apron flap from under shell. Pry off top shell and rinse away breathing ducts or lungs. Break or cut body in half, or cut large crabs into smaller pieces. Twist off claws, reserving pincers for garnish. Refrigerate until ready to use.

Soak mushrooms in hot water for about 20 minutes, then drain, squeezing to remove all liquid. Use shears or a small knife to cut away tough stems, and discard. Cut mushroom caps into thin julienne, then crosswise into small dice; set aside.

In a large pot, bring 6 cups (48 fl oz/1.5 L) reserved liquid from cooking crab, or stock if using precooked crab, to a boil. Peel asparagus, cut off about 1½ inches (4 cm) of tips and set aside. Chop remaining asparagus into thin rounds. Add asparagus tips to boiling liquid and cook for 2 minutes. Using a slotted spoon, transfer asparagus tips to a bowl. Whisk arrowroot and water mixture into soup. Add sliced asparagus. Bring to a gentle boil to thicken. Season with salt and pepper. Whisk in egg white. At the last minute, add crabmeat and mushrooms. Stir to combine and remove from heat. To serve, garnish with cilantro sprigs and reserved asparagus tips.

Serves 6

Note: This is a specialty of the mile-high city of Dalat, where it is made with thick-shelled mud crab transported by truck daily from the coast. The soup is especially popular in summer, when the crabs taste sweetest and render their juices best.

Ingredients

- 2 lb (1 kg) raw or cooked crab in its shell, or 1 lb (500 g) lump crabmeat, picked over for shell

- 25 dried black mushrooms

- 6 cups (48 fl oz/1.5 L) water, or if using precooked crab Quick Seafood Stock (page 118) or Fish Stock (page 118)

- 6 spears asparagus, trimmed

- 1 tablespoon arrowroot or cornstarch (cornflour) dissolved in 1 tablespoon water

- 1 teaspoon salt

- ½ teaspoon ground pepper

- 1 egg white

- ⅓ cup (½ oz/15 g) coarsely torn fresh cilantro (fresh coriander) sprigs

Ingredients

8 cups (64 fl oz/2 L) Enriched Meat Stock (page 118) or canned chicken broth

12 oz (375 g) boneless, skinless chicken thighs or breasts, thinly sliced

1 cup (6½ oz/200 g) uncooked rice, preferably jasmine rice (see Hints)

¼ cup (2 fl oz/60 ml) vegetable oil

½ cup (2 oz/60 g) thinly sliced brown or pink shallots (French shallots) (see Hints)

1 teaspoon ground pepper

¼ bunch (⅔ oz/20 g) Chinese (flat/garlic) chives, coarsely chopped

fish sauce to taste

Chicken and rice **soup**
Chao ga

In a large pot over high heat, bring stock or broth to a boil. Add chicken and cook, 1–2 minutes for breast meat or 2–3 minutes for thigh meat. Using a skimmer, transfer chicken to a bowl.

Meanwhile, rinse rice in several changes of cold water until water is no longer cloudy. Drain and gradually stir into boiling stock. Reduce heat to low and cook, uncovered and stirring occasionally, until just tender, about 15 minutes.

While rice is cooking, heat oil in a medium frying pan over medium-high heat until surface shimmers. Add shallots and cook, stirring constantly, until lightly golden and crisp, about 5 minutes. Using a slotted spoon, transfer to paper towels to drain.

At the last minute, add cooked chicken pieces to stock, stir to combine, then ladle into warmed soup bowls. Sprinkle with pepper and garnish with chives and fried shallots. Season to taste with fish sauce.

Serves 6

Hints: Although aged rice commands premium prices throughout much of Asia, this dish benefits from young, new-crop rice. Most Asian grocers carry rice clearly stamped with its season date.

Packaged crisply fried shallots, labeled "fried red onions," are a time-saving substitute for the fried onions used here. They are available at Asian markets.

Variation: With fish (Chao ca qua) Replace stock with Fish Stock (page 118) or Quick Seafood Stock (page 118) and substitute an equal quantity of fish fillets, cut into 1-inch (2.5-cm) pieces, for chicken pieces. Garnish with chives, plus ¼ cup (⅓ oz/10 g) coarsely chopped dill. Season to taste with fish sauce.

Ingredients

4 cups (18 oz/ 550g) Steamed Rice (page 120)

4 eggs

vegetable oil for cooking

2 large onions, coarsely chopped

4 oz (125 g) shelled shrimp (prawns), coarsely chopped

1½ cups (9 oz/280 g) diced cooked chicken meat, firmly packed

½ cup (4 fl oz/125 ml) fish sauce or to taste

¼ green bell pepper (capsicum), seeded and finely diced

¼ red bell pepper (capsicum), seeded and finely diced

2 teaspoons ground pepper

1 tablespoon Asian chili sauce or more to taste

cilantro (fresh coriander) sprigs for garnish

shrimp crackers for serving (optional)

Metropole fried rice
Com rang Metropole

Cold steamed rice cooks best in this recipe; if using freshly steamed rice, set the rice aside to cool slightly.

Prepare 4 thin omelets as described on page 121. Cool omelets slightly, roll, then cut into strips; set aside.

In a large frying pan or wok, heat 2 tablespoons oil over high heat and stir-fry onions until barely wilted, about 1 minute. Add shrimp and chicken, and stir-fry for 2 minutes. Season with half of fish sauce, add bell peppers, and stir-fry for 1 minute. Add rice, pepper, chili sauce and remaining fish sauce to taste. Reduce heat to medium-high and stir-fry for 5 minutes.

Moisten six individual rice bowls or small ramekins and pack with fried rice. Alternatively, press all rice into a lightly oiled 6-cup (1½-qt/ 1.5-L) bowl. Press firmly, then unmold into the middle of a plate. Sprinkle with omelet strips and cilantro. If desired, accompany with shrimp crackers.

Serves 6

Note: This is a signature dish of the Sofitel Metropole Hotel in Hanoi.

Shrimp fried rice, Hue style

Com Hue

Prepare silky pork sausage as directed on page 49, and dice.

Cook rice and keep warm.

Soak mushrooms in hot water for 20 minutes, then drain, squeezing to remove all liquid. Use scissors or a small knife to cut tough stems; discard. Cut mushroom caps into small dice and set aside. If using dried lotus seeds, soak in warm water for 20 minutes, then use a toothpick inserted from end to end to remove any bitter green sprouts.

Cook carrot in salted boiling water for 30 seconds. Using a slotted spoon, transfer to a bowl and let cool. Add lotus seeds to boiling water and cook for 20 minutes. Using a slotted spoon, transfer to a bowl. If shrimp are raw, plunge into same boiling water and cook until just pink, about 1 minute. Drain and coarsely chop all but 2 shrimp. Cut the 2 whole shrimp in half lengthwise and set aside.

In a wok or large frying pan, heat oil over medium-high heat. Add sausage, mushroom, lotus seeds, carrot, shrimp and onion, and stir-fry for 5 minutes. Stir in fish sauce, pepper, salt and all but 1 tablespoon chives.

Lightly oil an 8-cup (2-qt/2-L) bowl and firmly press one-third of hot rice into bowl. Add stir-fried ingredients, spreading to layer evenly, then add remaining two-thirds rice. Press to compact rice firmly, then unmold contents of bowl onto a plate. Garnish with reserved shrimp and reserved chives, cilantro sprigs and chili.

Serves 6–8

Hint: To save time, for silky pork sausage, substitute diced cooked pork loin or chicken breast or cooked sausage such as frankfurter or mortadella for silky pork sausage.

Ingredients

3 oz (90 g) Silky Pork Sausage (page 49) (see also Hint)

6 cups (27 oz/ 810 g) Steamed Rice (page 120)

6 dried black mushrooms

¼ cup (1½ oz/45 g) dried lotus seeds (optional)

1 carrot, peeled and diced

1 lb (500 g) shrimp (prawns), shelled and deveined, or 8 oz (250 g) shrimp (prawn) meat

2–3 tablespoons vegetable oil

1 small onion, diced

2 tablespoons fish sauce

¼ teaspoon ground pepper

½ teaspoon salt

¼ bunch Chinese (flat/garlic) chives, coarsely chopped, for garnish

cilantro (fresh coriander) sprigs for garnish

1 fresh long red chili, seeded and cut into thin strips for garnish

Ingredients

4 cups (18 oz/540 g) Steamed Rice (page 120)

25 dried black mushrooms

¼ cup (1½ oz/45 g) dried lotus seeds (optional)

3 tablespoons vegetable oil

2 cups (10 oz/300 g) diced cooked chicken meat, firmly packed

2 teaspoons salt

1 teaspoon ground pepper

2–3 scallions (shallots/spring onions), including green parts, coarsely chopped

2 tablespoons fish sauce

1–2 large fresh or dried lotus leaves (see Note)

Steamed rice in lotus parcels
Com rang hat sen

Cold steamed rice cooks best in this recipe; if using freshly steamed rice, set the rice aside to cool slightly.

Soak mushrooms in hot water for 20 minutes, then drain, squeezing to remove all liquid. Use scissors or a small knife to cut tough stems; discard. Cut mushroom caps into small dice and set aside. If using dried lotus seed, soak in warm water for 20 minutes, then use a toothpick inserted from end to end to remove any bitter green sprouts. Cook lotus seed in gently boiling water until tender, about 20 minutes; drain and set aside.

In a wok or large frying pan, heat 2 tablespoons of the oil over medium-high heat. Add mushroom, chicken and lotus seed, if using, and stir-fry for 5 minutes. Season with salt and pepper and transfer to bowl.

In same wok or pan, heat remaining 1 tablespoon of oil over medium-high heat and stir-fry rice and scallions for 5 minutes. Season with fish sauce. Add chicken and mushrooms and mix well.

If using a dried lotus leaf, cover it with boiling water to soften, then drain. The water will become brown and somewhat murky. Fresh leaves should be wiped to remove any grit or sediment.

Spread out leaf and pile steamed rice mixture in middle. Press lightly to compact the pile into a 10-x-7-inch (25-x-18-cm) mound, 2–3 inches (5–7 cm) high. Leave a 5-inch (13-cm) clearance on all sides. Fold the two sides over each other as if folding an envelope, leaving narrow ends still exposed. Fold one end over, then hold packet upright. Lightly press to compress rice, then fold remaining end over to enclose firmly. Tie packet securely both crosswise and lengthwise with coarse kitchen string. The dish can be prepared to this point up to 1 hour ahead, or 3–4 hours if refrigerated.

Place parcel in a steamer over rapidly boiling water. Cover and steam until heated throughout, about 5 minutes. (Refrigerated parcels will require 15–20 minutes of steaming.) Carefully remove from steamer. To serve, use scissors to cut open parcel, rolling back lotus for a decorative appearance.

Serves 6

Note: Large, voluptuous lotus leaves are imbued with a slight taste of chestnut. Fresh lotus is available from May to September in Southeast Asia, but dried leaves are more commonly sold overseas. If unavailable, don't enclose the rice mixture in a parcel but serve hot, directly from wok or pan.

Variation: For individual servings, use 6 lotus leaves and divide filling equally into 6 portions. Place 1 portion onto each leaf. Fold as above.

Fried glass noodles with fish or eel

Mien xao luon

In a medium bowl, combine fish or eel, fish sauce and pepper. Stir well and refrigerate until ready to use, at least 20 minutes.

Soak mushrooms in hot water for 20 minutes, then drain, squeezing to remove all liquid. Use scissors or a small knife to cut tough stems; discard. Cut mushroom caps into small dice and set aside.

Stack a few Vietnamese mint leaves together and roll tightly into a cylinder. Use a sharp knife to cut crosswise into thin shreds. Repeat with remaining leaves. Cut chives into 1½-inch (4-cm) pieces.

Prepare noodles as described on page 33. Using scissors, cut noodles to manageable lengths for serving.

Transfer fish to a plate, reserving marinade in bowl, and pat fish dry with paper towels. Heat oil in a wok or large frying pan over medium-high heat until it shimmers. Add one-third of the fish and stir-fry until almost crisp, 3–5 minutes. Transfer to paper towels to drain.

Reduce heat to medium, draining all but ¼ cup of the oil. Add remaining fish plus marinade and mushrooms, and stir-fry for 3 minutes. Then add noodles and stir-fry for 2 minutes. Finally, add chives, onion, garlic, bean sprouts, reserved fried fish and remaining marinade. Stir-fry for 1 minute and sprinkle with Vietnamese mint. Transfer to a serving plate, and garnish with the reserved crispy-fried fish and chilies. Serve with lemon wedges, and chili sauce if desired.

Serves 8

Note: This is a very old Hanoi recipe, and popular restaurants there specialize in eel dishes. Sturgeon is probably the closest in texture to eel, although tender catfish fillets, as well as oily garfish and smelt, can also be substituted. Spanish mackerel is another option.

Ingredients

1 lb (500 g) skinless fish or eel fillets (see Note), finely diced

2 tablespoons fish sauce

½ teaspoon ground pepper

12 dried black mushrooms

leaves from 2 large sprigs Vietnamese mint (rau ram) or spearmint

1 bunch Chinese (flat/garlic) chives

6½-oz (200-g) packet cellophane (bean thread) noodles

about 1 cup vegetable oil for frying

2 onions, thinly sliced

6 cloves garlic, crushed

2 cups (4 oz/125 g) bean sprouts, rinsed and drained

2 fresh long red chilies, seeded and cut into thin strips

2 lemons, cut into wedges

Asian chili sauce for serving (optional)

Ingredients

1-inch (2.5-cm) knob fresh turmeric, or 3 teaspoons ground turmeric

1¼ lb (625 g) boned pork leg, preferably hock, shank or knuckle (see Hint)

¼ cup fish sauce

2 tomatoes, quartered or cut into wedges

4 cups (32 fl oz/1 L) Enriched Meat Stock (page 118) or canned beef broth

2 carambolas (star fruits), preferably slightly unripe, cut into ¼-inch (6-mm) stars (optional)

1 tablespoon tamarind puree, or to taste

1 taro stem (Vietnamese rhubarb— bac ha/doc mung), about 4 oz (125 g)

salt to taste

12-oz (375-g) packet dried rice vermicelli (bun)

3 scallions (shallots/spring onions), including green parts, coarsely chopped

FOR ACCOMPANIMENTS

Soup Herbs (see Variation, page 50) including cilantro (fresh coriander) sprigs, Vietnamese mint (rau ram) and bean sprouts

fresh long red chilies, sliced

2 lemons, cut into wedges

Pork and noodles **in broth**

Bun bung

Using a pestle, pound turmeric in a mortar, or alternatively use a grater. Soak extracted juice and pulp in 1 tablespoon water, from 3–4 minutes up to a few hours; then strain. Wear gloves to prevent turmeric staining your skin.

Cut pork into 1-inch (2.5-cm) cubes. Retain any rind, as this enriches the broth. In a bowl, combine fish sauce, turmeric and pork. Toss to coat (use a spoon, as turmeric will stain your hands) and let stand for 1–2 hours.

Pour meat and marinade into a large pot. Add tomatoes and stock. Bring to a low boil, reduce heat to low and cover. Simmer until meat is tender, about 2½ hours. Add more water if it cooks dry. Add carambola if using, and tamarind puree to taste. (The carambola will slightly sour the broth, so add more tamarind judiciously.)

If using taro, peel stem by pulling upward at base. It should come away easily in ribbonlike strips; do not use a potato peeler. Cut taro into julienne, about 2 inches (5 cm) long. Lightly sprinkle with salt, leave for 5 minutes. Then press gently to remove any bitter juice. Rinse and press again, wipe with a damp cloth, then add to pot. Cook until barely tender, 2–3 minutes.

Prepare dried noodles as described on page 32, and set aside. Just before serving, plunge noodles momentarily into a pot of boiling water to reheat, drain immediately, and divide among 6 large soup bowls.

Ladle soup over noodles. Sprinkle with chopped scallions and serve, accompanied by soup herbs, chilies and lemon wedges.

Serves 6

Hint: For a quicker variation, use a tender pork cut such as fillet or tenderloin. Proceed as above, simmering gently until tender, about 20 minutes only.

TYSABRI®
(natalizumab)

Pho noodle soup with beef

Pho bo

Preheat oven to 400°F (200°C/Gas 6). Enclose ginger and shallots in a square of aluminum foil. Roast for about 20 minutes. Remove from foil, chop ginger and shallots, and add to stock in a large pot. Add star anise and cardamom. Bring stock to a boil, then reduce heat to low and simmer for at least 30 minutes. Set aside.

Prepare dried noodles as described on page 32. Fresh noodles, direct from the packet, can also be used.

Immediately before serving, remove star anise and cardamom from stock. Bring stock to a boil. Plunge noodles into boiling water for a moment to reheat, drain immediately and place in warmed individual bowls. Divide chives, scallions and onion among bowls. Toss meat into boiling stock, then ladle meat and boiling stock into each bowl. Accompany with soup herbs, chilies, fish sauce and lemon wedges. Squeeze wedges of lemon into individual bowls.

Serves 4–6

Note: Banh pho or rice noodles generally come in three widths, but noodles that are 1/8 inch (3 mm) wide are normally used for pho.

Variation: Pho with chicken (Pho ga) Omit star anise and cardamom, and replace beef with 2 large boneless, skinless chicken breast halves. Slice chicken very thinly and poach in simmering stock until opaque throughout, about 2 minutes.

Ingredients

1-inch (2.5-cm) knob fresh ginger, peeled

1/4 cup (1 oz/30 g) brown or pink shallots (French shallots), peeled

6 cups (48 fl oz/1.5 L) Enriched Meat Stock (page 118) or canned broth

1 star anise

1 brown or black cardamom pod, lightly crushed (see Ingredients, page 22)

1-lb (500-g) packet rice noodles or rice sticks

2 tablespoons coarsely chopped Chinese (flat/garlic) chives

2 scallions (shallots/spring onions), including green parts, coarsely chopped

1 small onion, thinly sliced

6 oz (180 g) beef rump (Scotch fillet) or eye of round (eye of silverside), sliced paper thin

FOR ACCOMPANIMENTS

Soup Herbs (See Variation, page 50), including eryngo (sawtooth coriander) leaves, peppermint and bean sprouts

2 fresh medium or long red chilies, cut into small rings

fish sauce or Nuoc Cham Sauce (page 116)

1–2 lemons, cut into wedges

Ingredients

3 lb (1.5 kg) raw jumbo shrimp (green king prawns), shelled and deveined, tails left on

1 tablespoon arrowroot or cornstarch (cornflour)

1–2 tablespoons sugar (optional)

about ½ cup (2 oz/60 g) cornstarch (cornflour)

vegetable oil for deep-frying

1 orange for garnish

cilantro (fresh coriander) sprigs for garnish

FOR ORANGE SAUCE

2 cups (16 fl oz/500 ml) freshly squeezed orange juice (about 5 oranges)

3 tablespoons fish sauce

Fried shrimp **with orange sauce**

Tom ran xot cam

To butterfly shrimp: Cut them deeply lengthwise along back, but not all the way through; gently score underside of shrimp to prevent curling. Cover and refrigerate until ready to use.

To make orange sauce: Pour orange juice into a non-reactive saucepan and bring to a boil. Continue boiling until slightly reduced, 5–10 minutes. In a small bowl, stir fish sauce and arrowroot together until dissolved, then stir this into boiling orange juice. Add sugar to taste if juice is too acidic. Set aside and keep warm.

Toss shrimp with cornstarch. In a wok or deep fryer, heat 4 inches (10 cm) oil to 350°F (180°C) and fry one-third of shrimp at a time until crisp and golden brown, 2–3 minutes (see Caution.) Using a slotted spoon, transfer to paper towels to drain. Keep warm in a low oven while cooking successive batches.

To serve, cut orange for garnish in half, then thinly slice each half into half-moon slices. Arrange slices around sides of a serving plate and spoon some of sauce into center of plate. Place fried shrimp in center, and place any remaining sauce in an accompanying bowl. Sprinkle with cilantro sprigs.

Serves 4–6

Hint: If using frozen shrimp, thaw in the refrigerator prior to using.

Caution: When deep-frying, make sure the wok or deep fryer is never filled more than one-third full, as the oil can froth up to double its volume when food is added, and any spilled oil can catch on fire.

Sautéed squid with leeks

Muc xao toi tay

Ingredients

1 lb (500 g) cleaned squid (calamari) (see Hint)

3 tablespoons fish sauce

½ teaspoon ground pepper

2 large leeks or 6 baby leeks, white part only, well rinsed

4 scallions (shallots/spring onions), including green parts, chopped

3 tablespoons vegetable oil

3 small tomatoes, quartered or sectioned

1 onion, coarsely chopped

⅓-inch (1-cm) knob fresh ginger, peeled and cut into fine julienne

1 tablespoon cornstarch (cornflour) or arrowroot dissolved in 1 tablespoon water

Steamed Rice (page 120) for serving

Marinate squid in 2 tablespoons fish sauce and pepper.

Cut leeks and scallions into fine julienne.

In a large frying pan, heat oil over high heat and sauté squid for 1 minute. Add leeks, tomatoes, onion, ginger and scallions. Stir-fry for 2 minutes, then add cornstarch and water mixture. Stir well, then reduce heat to low, cover, and simmer for 3 minutes. Stir in remaining 1 tablespoon fish sauce. Serve hot with steamed rice.

Serves 6

Notes: Do not overcook squid as it becomes tough and rubbery.

In Hanoi, young leeks are so tender, they are often eaten raw in salads.

Hint: Uncleaned squid If using uncleaned squid, increase proportion accordingly. To clean, pull tentacles and head from the tubelike body. Cut directly behind eyes to free tentacles from eyes. Use two fingers to pull out plastic-like cartilage and innards, and discard. Rinse and reserve tentacles and tubes. If small, cut squid bodies in half or quarters, and larger squid into 1-x-2-inch (2.5-x-5-cm) pieces.

To tenderize and beautify larger squid, lightly score inside of flesh with a sharp knife, making a lattice pattern. This works best with larger bodies, as small squid are thin.

Ingredients

3 rock lobster tails, halved lengthwise, about 6 oz (180 g) each

FOR ROUGAIL SAUCE

½-inch (1.2-cm) knob fresh turmeric, peeled, or 2 teaspoons ground turmeric

5 garlic cloves, crushed in a garlic press

2 tablespoons finely chopped brown or pink shallots (French shallots)

1 fresh long red chili, seeded and finely chopped

2 stalks lemongrass, white part only, peeled and finely chopped

2 tablespoons fish sauce

juice of 1 lime

3 tablespoons vegetable or olive oil

1 teaspoon ground pepper

FOR ACCOMPANIMENTS

Nuoc Cham Sauce (page 116) or Simple Fish Sauce (page 114)

1–2 lemons or limes, quartered or cut into wedges

1 fresh long red or green chili, seeded and thinly sliced

cilantro (fresh coriander) sprigs

sweet Vietnamese pickles (optional) (see page 53 and 58)

Grilled lobster tails with rougail sauce
Tom hum nuong xot cay

To make sauce: If using fresh turmeric, pound in a mortar using a pestle, or alternatively use a grater. Soak extracted juice and pulp in 1 tablespoon water, from 3–4 minutes up to a few hours; then strain. Wear gloves to prevent turmeric staining your skin. Combine turmeric mixture or ground turmeric and all remaining sauce ingredients. Alternatively, instead of chopping each ingredient separately, combine all sauce ingredients in a food processor, and puree.

Rinse lobster halves and pat dry. Place in sauce and let stand for 1 hour, turning occasionally to coat all sides.

Prepare a charcoal grill (barbecue) or brazier following directions on page 18, or preheat an oven broiler (grill). Cook lobster, turning once and spooning additional marinade atop occasionally during cooking, until opaque throughout, about 10 minutes without shell and about 12 minutes with shell. If broiling (grilling), cook lobster, flesh-side up, about 4 inches (10 cm) from heat source, for 10–15 minutes.

Place lobster on serving plate. Serve hot with nuoc cham sauce or simple fish sauce, lemon or lime wedges, chili slices, cilantro sprigs and sweet pickles.

Serves 6

Note: Rougail is a generic French term applied to any number of spicy sauces, especially those served in tropical countries.

Ingredients

⅓ cup (3 fl oz/90 ml) dry rice wine or dry sherry

3 tablespoons fish sauce

1 teaspoon sugar

2 teaspoons ground pepper

2 lb (1 kg) boneless beef blade or chuck, trimmed and cut into 1-inch (2.5-cm) cubes (see Hint, page 87)

3 tablespoons vegetable oil

½ cup (2 oz/60 g) brown or pink shallots (French shallots), crushed

cloves from ½ bulb garlic, crushed

2 sticks cinnamon, or ½ teaspoon ground cinnamon

½ teaspoon aniseed

about 1¼ cups (10 fl oz/310 ml) water

3 tomatoes, peeled and seeded

¼ cup (2 oz/60 g) butter

¼ cup (1 oz/30 g) all-purpose (plain) flour

cilantro (fresh coriander) sprigs for garnish (optional)

crusty bread rolls or baguette for serving

Step-by-step Beef braised in rice wine
Bo xot vang

1. In a glass or earthenware bowl, combine rice wine, fish sauce, sugar and 1 teaspoon pepper. Stir to blend. Add beef and let stand at room temperature for 2 hours, or cover and refrigerate for up to 24 hours. Stir several times during this period. Using a slotted spoon, transfer beef from marinade and pat dry; reserve marinade.

2. In a large, heavy pot or Dutch oven, heat oil over medium heat and sauté half of shallots and half of garlic until soft, about 3 minutes. Using a slotted spoon, transfer to a bowl. Add half of beef to pot and cook, stirring frequently, until all sides are lightly seared, about 5 minutes. Using a slotted spoon, transfer to a bowl. Repeat with remaining meat.

In same pot, combine meat, cinnamon, aniseed and cooked shallots and add remaining garlic. Add 1 cup (8 fl oz/250 ml) water plus any marinade. Cover and simmer over medium-low heat just until beef is tender, about 2 hours. Shake occasionally to prevent scorching. If the braise cooks dry, add a little more water.

3. Meanwhile, peel and seed tomatoes: Use a small knife to cut away and remove each tomato core. Turn tomato over and lightly score

1

2

3

4

underside with an X. Plunge into a large pot of rapidly boiling water and cook for exactly 10 seconds. Remove immediately from water and plunge into ice water to stop cooking. The skin should now pull easily from pulp; discard. Cut tomatoes in half and squeeze over a strainer to extract all seeds. Discard seeds and retain tomatoes and juice.

4. In a medium saucepan, combine tomatoes, strained tomato juice and remaining raw shallots, garlic and 1 teaspoon pepper. Add remaining ¼ cup (2 fl oz/60 ml) water and cook until tomatoes are just starting to break up, about 3 minutes. In a separate saucepan, melt butter over low heat and whisk in flour. Cook, stirring constantly, until it barely begins to brown, about 2–3 minutes. Whisk into tomato mixture and remove from heat.

When beef is barely tender, remove cinnamon sticks, if using, from braise. Stir in tomato mixture. Reduce heat to a simmer, cover, and cook until fork tender, 30–60 minutes. If desired, garnish with cilantro sprigs. Serve with bread rolls or baguette.

Serves 4

Note: This is a classic example of Vietnamese fusion food, created, presumably, after the French colonists' departure, when red wine flowed less freely and the local substitute of rice wine was used. This recipe's European prototype is arguably boeuf bourguignon or a Flemish-style carbonnade.

Hint: Inexpensive beef cuts work best in this braised dish. Do not use premium cuts like loin (saddle), or lean meat like round (topside), as they can become tough and dry during long, slow cooking.

Ingredients

FOR MARINADE

3 tablespoons ground turmeric, or a 3-inch (7.5-cm) knob fresh turmeric, peeled and chopped

1-inch (2.5-cm) knob fresh galingal or ginger, peeled

1–2 fresh long red chilies, seeded

2 tablespoons fish sauce

¼ cup (2 fl oz/60 ml) water

1 tablespoon rice vinegar or distilled white vinegar

1 tablespoon sugar, or more to taste

1 lb (500 g) skinless catfish fillets (see Note), cut into bite-sized pieces

5-oz (150-g) packet dried rice vermicelli (bun), softened (see page 32) and cut into manageable lengths for serving

¼ cup (2 fl oz/60 ml) vegetable oil

1 bunch dill, stemmed and cut into 1½-inch (4-cm) lengths

4 scallions (shallots), including green parts, coarsely chopped

½ cup (2 oz/60 g) thinly sliced brown or pink shallots (French shallots)

2 cloves garlic, thinly sliced

⅓ cup (2 oz/60 g) chopped peanuts, lightly toasted (see Hint, page 55) and chopped

FOR ACCOMPANIMENTS

Table Greens (page 50), including whole butter (Boston) lettuce leaves

1 cup (8 fl oz/250 ml) Nuoc Cham Sauce (page 116)

¼ cup (2 fl oz/60 ml) Fermented Shrimp Dipping Sauce (page 117) (optional)

Cha ca fish with turmeric
Cha ca la vong

To make marinade: In a mortar, using a pestle, pound turmeric, galingal and chili to a paste. Alternatively, process in a blender or food processor. Add all remaining marinade ingredients and stir until dissolved. Pour into a bowl. Add fish, toss to coat, and refrigerate for 3 hours. Meanwhile, prepare dried noodles as described on page 32.

Transfer fish to a plate, scrape off marinade and reserve, and pat fish dry with paper towels. To give fish a distinct smoky flavor, it is first grilled then fried, but the grilling is optional. If grilling, prepare a charcoal grill (barbecue) or brazier following directions on page 18 and place fish in a grilling basket. Alternatively, preheat an oven broiler (grill). Cook until opaque throughout, 3–4 minutes.

In a medium frying pan, heat oil over medium-high heat until surface shimmers. Add cooked or raw fish, a few pieces at a time, to hot oil, stirring carefully so as not to break up pieces. Cook until flaky to the touch but not crisp, 1–3 minutes. Using a skimmer, transfer to a platter. Repeat with remaining fish. Reduce heat to medium, add dill and scallions to pan, and stir-fry just until wilted. Place these atop cooked fish. Quickly stir-fry shallots and garlic in same pan, with any reserved marinade, and spoon atop. Finally, top with crushed peanuts.

To serve, lay out a lettuce leaf, top with some rice noodles plus assorted table greens, and add a spoonful of cooked fish. Fold lettuce leaf into a small parcel and eat with your hands. Dip into nuoc cham sauce, and, if desired, a very small spoonful of fermented shrimp dipping sauce. Use sparingly: its flavor is pungent, and an acquired taste. In Vietnam, this is accompanied with sesame-topped rice crackers.

Serves 4

Note: Ca bong lau and ca lang, varieties of catfish, are used for this dish in Vietnam. Trout substitutes well, as do pike and salmon. Asian alternatives include deep-sea mullet and Taiwanese milk fish.

Braised pork with young coconut

Lon kho nuoc dua

Ingredients

- 1½ lb (750 g) boneless pork shank, leg or shoulder, cut into 1-inch (2.5-cm) cubes
- ⅓ cup (3 oz/90 g) sugar
- 2 coconuts, preferably young coconuts, or about 4 cups (32 fl oz/1 L) coconut water (see Hint)
- 2 tablespoons vegetable oil
- ⅔ cup (5 fl oz/150 ml) fish sauce
- 6 hard-boiled eggs, shelled
- 1 fresh long red or green chili, seeded and thinly sliced
- ⅓ cup (½ oz/15 g) coarsely chopped Chinese (flat/garlic) chives
- 6 scallions (shallots/spring onions), including green parts, cut into 1-inch (2.5-cm) pieces

Place pork in a medium casserole dish. Sprinkle with sugar and refrigerate for 1 hour. Traditionally, any rind is retained to enrich the juices, but discard if preferred.

Pierce top of coconuts and drain coconut water; you need about 4 cups (32 fl oz/1 L). If using young coconuts, use a large knife to cut away the top of the coconut (the shell of young coconuts is not as hard as that of older ones). Scoop gelatinous flesh from inside shell and cut into small dice; set aside.

In a medium pot, heat oil over medium heat and cook pork, stirring, until lightly golden on all sides, 3–5 minutes. You may need to do this in 2 batches to prevent crowding. If meat begins to burn because of sugar, add 1–2 tablespoons coconut water. Add fish sauce and remaining coconut water, and, if using, coconut meat. Bring to a low boil, then immediately reduce heat to low, partially cover, and very gently simmer until pork is tender and liquid reduced by half, about 2–2½ hours. Add hard-boiled eggs to the pot for last 30 minutes of cooking time. Serve garnished with chili, chives and scallions.

Serves 6

Notes: This is a southern Vietnamese recipe, popularly sold on the streets of Ho Chi Minh City (Saigon).

Cook very slowly to ensure tender results.

Hint: Coconut water is not coconut milk, but the watery liquid inside a coconut. While coconut water from older coconuts can be used, try to find young coconuts or packaged coconut water (nuoc dua tuoi). Often, the water is lightly sweetened. If so, omit sugar. Alternatively, the separated clear liquid layer in canned coconut milk can be used. (See also page 119.)

Ingredients

1 duck (about 3 lb/1.5 kg) or duck pieces (see Hint, page 93)

½ cup (2 oz/60 g) finely chopped brown or pink shallots (French shallots)

6 cloves garlic, finely chopped

about ½ teaspoon ground pepper

2 tablespoons fish sauce

2–3 tablespoons vegetable oil

3 cups (24 fl oz/750 ml) Enriched Meat Stock (page 118), Chicken Stock (page 118) or canned beef or chicken broth

2 tablespoons distilled rice alcohol or vodka

1 fresh pineapple, peeled, or one 28-oz (850-g) can pineapple rings, drained

1 tablespoon sugar

1 teaspoon salt or to taste

1 tablespoon arrowroot or cornstarch (cornflour) mixed with 1 tablespoon water

cilantro (fresh coriander) sprigs for garnish

coarsely ground pepper to taste

Step-by-step Braised duck with pineapple
Vit nau dua

1. If using whole duck, begin by placing duck on a cutting board. Pull each leg away from body and use a cleaver or large chef's knife to cut through the joint attaching it to the body. Likewise, pull each wing away from body and cut through its joint. Cut duck carcass in half lengthwise by cutting through bones connecting breast and back. Remove and discard any large bones as necessary. Now cut down along backbone, turn over duck, and cut lengthwise through breastbone. You should have 8 pieces. Cut each section crosswise through the bones into bite-sized pieces.

2. In a large bowl, toss duck pieces with shallots, garlic, pepper and fish sauce. Let stand at room temperature for 1 hour or refrigerate overnight. Using a slotted spoon, transfer duck to a plate, reserving marinade. Pat duck dry with paper towels.

3. In a large frying pan or heavy pot, heat oil over medium heat. Add duck pieces, skin-side down, and cook until golden brown and all fat has been extracted, about 15–20 minutes. Drain off and discard fat. For a lighter, skin-free version, refer to the hint below.

4. Transfer duck to a heavy pot. Add stock, liquor and reserved marinade. Bring to a very gentle boil, then immediately reduce heat to

1

2

3

4

low, cover, and cook at a bare simmer until tender, 20 minutes.

5. Meanwhile, cut fresh pineapple in half lengthwise, then into half-moons ½inch (1.2 cm) thick. Use a small paring knife to remove core. Alternatively, cut canned pineapple rings in half crosswise. In a large, nonstick frying pan over medium heat, lightly brown pineapple pieces, sprinkling with sugar to create a light caramel glaze. Alternatively, use a large frying pan oiled with 1 tablespoon vegetable oil or butter, or vegetable oil cooking spray. Remove from heat and set aside.

6. When duck is almost done, add pineapple and taste for seasoning, adding salt to taste. Cook for a few minutes for flavors to meld. Using a slotted spoon, transfer duck and pineapple to a bowl; cover to keep warm. Strain cooking liquid. If liquid appears greasy, lightly float paper towels on the surface to absorb fat.

7. Add arrowroot mixture to sauce. Bring to a boil, stirring. Spoon some of this sauce over duck pieces. Serve additional sauce alongside. Garnish with cilantro sprigs and, sprinkle with coarsely ground pepper.

Serves 4

Note: Although it originated in the imperial capital of Hue, in the center of the country, this dish is now popular throughout Vietnam.

Hint: For a lighter version, use skinless duck pieces. Fry duck pieces until lightly browned, for only 2–3 minutes. Likewise, boneless, skinless duck breast can be used; simmer until just tender, 10–15 minutes.

Variation: Braised duck with orange Substitute an equal quantity of peeled orange segments for pineapple.

5

6

7

Finished recipe

Main Dishes

Ingredients

4 tablespoons (2 oz/60 g) sugar

4 tablespoons (2 fl oz/60 ml) water

1 lb (500 g) fresh side pork (pork belly), rind removed, cut into slices (rashers) about ¼ inch (6 mm) thick

1 lb (500 g) lean ground pork, preferably butt (leg) or shoulder

½ cup (4 fl oz/125 ml) fish sauce

½ cup (2 oz/60 g) finely chopped brown or pink shallots (French shallots)

½ bunch Chinese (flat/garlic) chives, coarsely chopped

1 tablespoon ground pepper

FOR ACCOMPANIMENTS

about 4 cups (32 fl oz/1 L) Nuoc Cham Sauce (page 116)

Table Greens (page 50), including whole butter (Boston) lettuce leaves

10 oz (300 g) dried rice vermicelli (bun), softened (see page 32) and cut into manageable lengths for serving

Hanoi bun cha
Bun cha

Prepare a caramel sauce by combining 2 tablespoons sugar and 2 tablespoons water in a small saucepan. Swirl over high heat to dissolve, but do not stir. Bring to a rapid boil and continue boiling until the color turns to a golden brown, 4–5 minutes. Immediately remove from heat and add remaining 2 tablespoons water to stop further caramelizing. Take care, lest the caramel spatter. Set aside to cool.

Cut pork slices in half, crosswise. Place sliced and ground pork in separate bowls. Pour half of cooled caramel onto pork in each bowl. (If caramel has solidified, add some fish sauce and return to heat briefly to melt.) Equally divide shallots, chives, fish sauce, pepper and remaining 2 tablespoons sugar between bowls. Toss to coat pork and let stand at room temperature for 2 hours, or cover and refrigerate overnight. Meanwhile, prepare dried noodles as described on page 32.

Prepare a charcoal grill (barbecue) or brazier following directions on page 18, or preheat an oven broiler (grill) with the cooking rack set about 5 inches (12 cm) from the heat source.

Remove both meats from marinade, draining any excess liquid. Wipe marinade solids from pork slices and add these solids to ground meat. Mix ground meat and marinade solids well, and form into small patties about 2 inches (5 cm) wide and ½ inch (1.2 cm) thick. Cook pork strips and patties, turning once, until sides are slightly charred and meat is cooked through, about 5 minutes.

Serve with individual bowls of nuoc cham sauce. The meat should be dipped into bowls and left to marinate for up to several minutes. Remove meat from sauce, enfold in a torn lettuce leaf with herbs and noodles, and eat using your hands.

Serves 6

Note: This is a classic street food of Hanoi, particularly popular at lunch.

Ingredients

Sizzling coconut crepes
Banh xeo

To make batter: In a medium bowl, sift rice starch, turmeric, curry powder and salt together. In another medium bowl, whisk egg, coconut milk and water together. Gradually stir into dry ingredients. You will have a very thin slurry. Stir in thinly sliced scallions.

In a medium bowl, combine pork with fish sauce, pepper and half of coarsely chopped scallions. Stir to blend well. In a large frying pan, heat 2–3 tablespoons oil over high heat and add pork mixture. Cook, stirring constantly, for 2–3 minutes. Using a slotted spoon, transfer to paper towels to drain.

Cut shrimp in half lengthwise. Heat the oil remaining in pan used to cook pork over high heat. If using raw shrimp, sauté until pink, about 2 minutes. If using precooked shrimp, sauté until heated through, about 1 minute. Using a slotted spoon, transfer to a bowl.

In a small nonstick or seasoned skillet about 8 inches (20 cm) in diameter, heat up to 1 tablespoon oil over medium to medium-high heat until surface shimmers. Add about ⅓ cup (3 fl oz/90 ml) batter and immediately tilt to evenly coat bottom of pan (see Notes).

After about 1 minute, when crepe begins to feel firm when gently pried from side, gently lift up and spoon up to 1 tablespoon oil directly onto pan. The oil should lightly sizzle. Tilt pan to distribute evenly. (This helps to achieve an even crisper, albeit slightly oily, crepe.) Top one side of crepe with about 1 tablespoon each of cooked pork and shrimp, plus sprouts and remaining coarsely chopped scallions. Fold crepe in half, cover the pan, reduce heat to low and cook for 2 minutes on each side. Carefully remove crepe to a serving plate. (If desired, lay a cut piece of banana leaf between crepes to prevent sticking.) Repeat with remaining batter and ingredients to make 12 crepes.

To serve, tear off a bit of crepe and its filling, wrap in a piece of lettuce with herbs, plus a piece of rice paper, then dip into the desired sauce. Traditionally, this dish is accompanied by fermented shrimp sauce; its taste is very strong.

Makes 12 crepes (serves 4–6)

Notes: Achieving the correct initial temperature is a bit tricky, but once you master it, subsequent crepes will be easy. Be careful that the pan is not too hot, lest it cooks batter too quickly; conversely, too low a heat prevents sufficient adhesiveness.

The size of the crepe identifies the locale: In Vietnam's imperial capital of Hue, banh khoai crepes are cooked in small skillets about 6 inches (15 cm) in diameter, and they are also made without egg or coconut milk. Variations of this dish are also known throughout Cambodia.

Hint: Do not mistake Asian rice starch (bot gao te/bot te tinh khiet) for Western rice flour or powder, which is made from finely ground whole rice grains. Confusingly, most Asian rice starch packets are marketed under the name "rice flour." Rice starch feels silky to the touch and is made from long-grain ground rice amylose (the soluble portion of the rice grain). In this recipe, do not use a seemingly similar variety made from sticky (glutinous) rice. Its properties differ markedly; packets are usually labeled clearly to differentiate the two. Alternatively, "prepared crepe flour" (bot banh xeo) is also available at many Asian markets. It is a mixture of rice, mung bean and wheat starches. Another option for this recipe is to use a blend of rice starch and potato starch called bot banh cuon ("steamed rice rolls flour"). It is made in the US and is now marketed overseas.

Variations: In a wok In some regions, larger crepes are prepared in a wok, though this is tricky. Heat wok, add oil and ½ cup (4 fl oz/125 ml) batter, tilting to coat wok evenly. Once crepe is set, lift up crepe carefully on one side and spoon another 1 tablespoon oil between wok and crepe. Add filling, cover pan, and cook over low heat for about 3 minutes. Fold crepe in half, and cook, uncovered, for another 1 minute to crisp.

Step-by-step Preparing a fire pot or steamboat

1

2

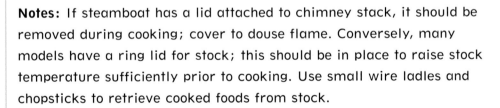

3

1. Prepare charcoals as descibed on page 18.

2. Pour hot stock into a doughnut-shaped fire pot or steamboat. Always add liquid to a fire pot or steamboat prior to heating with hot coals, lest the solder joints of some models overheat and cause leakage. Stock should fill about two-thirds of pot. At this point, use tongs to add hot coals to center of chimney pot, filling no more than halfway up. Allow stock to boil gently. (See Caution.)

3. Cooking meats and vegetables in stock results in an enriched soup. After guests have finished eating meat and vegetables, add steamed rice or, as here, noodles. Heat throughout: Rice noodles are ready when soft; fresh wheat or egg noodles within 2–3 minutes; and dried noodles can take up to 7 minutes, depending on thickness. Alternatively, precook noodles and then reheat in soup pot at the table. Ladle soup and noodles into soup bowls (see Notes).

Notes: If steamboat has a lid attached to chimney stack, it should be removed during cooking; cover to douse flame. Conversely, many models have a ring lid for stock; this should be in place to raise stock temperature sufficiently prior to cooking. Use small wire ladles and chopsticks to retrieve cooked foods from stock.

Sour broth, such as that used in Sour Steamboat Lau (page 99), is too acidic for soup.

Cautions: Never place a coal-heated pot directly on a table, (here we use a marble surface). It will char wood or melt plastic, and may shatter other materials such as glass. Place atop a fireproof base such as bricks or a stone slab. If there is a likelihood that the heat will conduct through the bricks onto the table, reinforce with a fireproof mat. Some electrical pots require similar prevention.

When burning any form of charcoal, always ensure that the room is well ventilated. Otherwise, carbon monoxide poisoning may occur.

Sour steamboat lau

Bo nhung dam

Arrange meat attractively on a platter or on individual plates in a single layer, overlapping as little as possible. Sprinkle meat with pepper and cover with plastic wrap and refrigerate until ready to serve, up to several hours in advance.

Arrange table greens on a platter. Cover and refrigerate until ready to serve, up to several hours in advance.

If using, soften rice paper sheets following directions on page 34.

To make soup stock: In a large saucepan, combine all stock ingredients and bring just to a boil, reduce heat to low and simmer until needed. Please note that some rice vinegars, especially Japanese brands, are slightly sweet; taste stock before adding extra 1 tablespoon sugar. Strain broth into a fire pot or metal fondue pot on the table. (See previous page for instructions.) The broth should fill the pot about two-thirds full; if not, add boiling water to the desired depth. At the table, bring to a rapid simmer.

To serve, lay a sheet of rice paper on a plate and top with a lettuce leaf and a few herbs. Take a piece of meat and drop it into simmering liquid for about 10 seconds, or until done as desired. Using a skimmer or chopsticks, retrieve meat and place it on lettuce leaf and herbs. Sprinkle with 1 teaspoon peanuts, then fold to enclose bottom and top. Roll up, as with spring rolls (see Hint). The finished result should be the size of a thick cigar, about 1 inch (2.5 cm) wide and 4 inches (10 cm) long. Dip in nuoc cham sauce and eat with your fingers.

Serves 6

Hint: If papers tear during rolling, fold sheets in half to a double thickness, and roll, leaving two ends exposed. Alternatively, omit rice paper sheets altogether, rolling meat and herbs in a lettuce leaf.

Ingredients

3 lb (1.5 kg) eye of round, sirloin or tenderloin (fillet), trimmed and sliced paper thin

2 teaspoons ground pepper

Table Greens (page 50), including butter (Boston) lettuce and dill sprigs

40 sheets dried rice papers, softened (see page 34) (optional)

FOR SOUP STOCK

2 cloves garlic, thinly sliced

1-inch (2.5-cm) knob fresh ginger, thinly sliced

1 stalk lemongrass, white section only, cut into thin rounds (optional)

1 cup (8 fl oz/250 ml) rice vinegar or distilled white vinegar

about 5 cups (40 fl oz/1.25 L) water

1 tablespoon salt

3–4 tablespoons sugar to taste

FOR ACCOMPANIMENTS

about 1 cup (4 oz/125 g) peanuts, lightly toasted and ground (see Hint, page 55)

Nuoc Cham Sauce (page 116)

Ingredients

FOR MEAT AND SEAFOOD PLATTERS

2 boneless, skinless chicken breast halves, thinly sliced

8 oz (250 g) beef, such as flank (skirt), thinly sliced across the grain

5 oz (150 g) each pork heart and kidney, trimmed and thinly sliced (optional)

8 oz (250 g) squid (calamari), cleaned (see Hint, page 83)

5 oz (150 g) fish fillets, cut into 1-inch (2.5-cm) pieces

5 oz (150 g) shelled and deveined raw jumbo shrimp (green king prawns)

FOR VEGETABLE PLATTER

¼ head Chinese (napa) cabbage

1½ cups (3 oz/90 g) bean sprouts, rinsed and drained

½ bunch spinach (English spinach), stemmed and well rinsed

1 basket (punnet) cherry tomatoes, stemmed and halved

1 bunch scallions (shallots/spring onions), including green parts, cut into 2-inch (5-cm) pieces

2 carambolas (star fruits) (optional), cut into stars ¼ inch (6 mm) thick

FOR SOUP STOCK

4–6 cups Chicken Stock (page 118) or canned chicken broth

⅓ cup (3 fl oz/90 ml) dry rice wine or dry sherry (optional)

12 dried black mushrooms, rinsed

FOR ACCOMPANIMENTS

Nuoc Cham Sauce (page 116)

Steamed Rice (page 120), (optional)

5 oz (150 g) thin egg or wheat noodles

Hanoi fire pot
Lau thap cam

For meat and seafood platters: Arrange sliced chicken, meat and seafood attractively on separate platters in a single layer, overlapping as little as possible. Cover with plastic wrap and refrigerate until ready to serve.

For vegetable platter: Cut away core from cabbage and discard, then cut cabbage quarter into half crosswise. Arrange all vegetables (except mushrooms for soup stock) decoratively on a platter. Cover with plastic wrap and refrigerate until ready to serve.

To make soup stock: In a large saucepan, combine stock and wine, if using. Bring to a boil, add mushrooms. Allow mushrooms to cook for at least 20 minutes, or until tender, before consuming. When eating, discard stems. Pour into a steamboat or electric saucepan or skillet (frying pan). If using a coal-fired pot or steamboat, follow directions on page 98, adding stock prior to adding coals. Maintain at a gentle boil. Have guests individually cook their meats and vegetables to desired degree, using small wire ladles, chopsticks or skewers. Foods will cook in 10 seconds to 3 minutes, depending on thickness. Spinach cooks in 10 seconds. Add more water or stock as necessary.

Accompany with small individual dipping bowls of nuoc cham sauce. Optionally, serve individual bowls of steamed rice, allowing juices from cooked meats and sauces to flavor rice. When guests have finished meat and vegetables, add noodles to soup pot. Fresh noodles cook in 2 minutes, while dried noodles take up to 7 minutes, depending on thickness and variety used. Ladle out bowls of soup and noodles for each diner.

Serves 6

Note: Thap cam means "with everything"; consequently, this fondue contains numerous meat and fish varieties. Chicken stock is the most versatile stock for such combination steamboats, but use fish stock when cooking only fish and shellfish (plus vegetables) and beef stock when cooking beef and organ meat (offal) fondues.

Ingredients

11 oz (330 g) canned lychees
(litchis) in syrup (see Notes)

¼ cup (½ oz/15 g) candied
(crystallized) ginger, chopped

⅔ cup (5 fl oz/150 ml) water

2 teaspoons freshly squeezed lemon
or lime juice

mint sprigs for garnish

SWEETS

Ginger and lychee **granita**
Kem trai vai voi gung

Pour lychees and their syrup into a blender or food processor (see Notes). Add ginger, water and lemon juice, then process until coarsely pureed.

Pour into a shallow pan or ice tray and place in freezer. Stir every 15 minutes until mixture freezes.

To serve, use a heavy spoon to scrape granita crystals into a bowl. Garnish with mint sprigs.

Serves 4–6

Notes: Most canned lychees are already pitted; if not, cut away and discard seed from each fruit before pureeing.

To use fresh lychees, remove both peel and pit, and add ½ cup (4 fl oz/125 ml) Sugar Syrup (page 108).

Hints: Candied ginger comes both crystallized and in syrup; both varieties suit this recipe. If in season, mild-tasting young ginger, with a pale, parchmentlike skin, can replace the candied rhizome. Older ginger, with a darker, thicker skin, does not suit as it is more fibrous and stronger tasting.

Granita is a sweetened ice, coarser in texture than sherbet (sorbet) or ice cream. If using an ice cream machine, add ½ egg white to mixture and process as above. The texture will be lighter in both color and texture.

Ingredients

1 cup (7 oz/220 g) dried small black beans or black-eyed peas (beans) (see Ingredients, page 20)

8 cups (64 fl oz/2 L) water for cooking

1 tablespoon arrowroot or tapioca starch

1 cup (8 oz/250 g) sugar

crushed ice

Sweet black bean "soup"

Che dau den

Pre-soaking beans: If using black beans or black eyed peas (beans), soak the beans overnight, or for at least four hours. Alternatively, for a quick soaking method, place the beans in a medium pot with a tight fitting lid. Cover with water, bring to the boil, uncovered, for 1 minute. Remove from the heat, cover tightly and rest for 1 hour. Drain before using.

In a large pot, combine beans and water. Bring to a boil, reduce heat and simmer until beans are barely tender, up to 1½ hours. (Surprisingly, tiny Vietnamese black beans cook much slower than other beans, yet still retain crunchiness).

Take a spoonful or so of cooking juices and stir into arrowroot, then return to pot. Add sugar and stir to dissolve. Remove from heat and let cool. Refrigerate until chilled, at least 2 hours. Spoon beans and juice into individual glasses or cups, add some crushed ice and serve.

Serves 6

Note: Sweetened condensed milk can be used to sweeten this recipe.

Hints: Substitute black gram (sabat urad) for beans, available at Asian markets, some natural foods stores, and Indian markets. If using black gram, do not presoak, and cook for about 30 minutes only.

Sweet gingered rice

Che con ong

Ingredients

1 cup (6½ oz/200 g) uncooked sticky (glutinous) rice

½ cup (4 oz/125 g) raw sugar or palm sugar, preferably dark

1-inch (2.5-cm) knob fresh ginger, peeled and finely grated

½ cup (2 oz/60 g) fresh or dried (desiccated) grated coconut (see Note)

2 tablespoons chopped peanuts, lightly toasted (see Hint, page 55)

Soak rice in water to cover for at least 3 hours and preferably for 8 hours; drain. Pour into a conical bamboo steamer or steamer basket lined with cheesecloth (muslin). Set over a pot of boiling water, cover, and steam until tender, about 20 minutes. Turn out rice into a medium bowl. Cover and keep warm.

In a small saucepan over high heat, combine sugar and ¾ cup water. Stir until dissolved, then boil for 1 minute. Add ginger. Reduce heat and barely simmer for 5 minutes. Pour syrup over cooked rice. Stir lightly until rice is just coated. As it will set while cooling, spoon rice immediately into small individual bowls or molds. Alternatively, flatten into a tray or plate, and cut into large 1¼-inch (3-cm) cubes. Serve at room temperature, garnished with coconut and peanuts.

Serves 4–6

Note: If using fresh coconut, see page 119 for preparation. You will only need a small quantity for this recipe, so wrap and refrigerate remainder for another use, such as to make Coconut Milk (page 119).

Sweet mung bean cake **with sesame**

Che kho

Ingredients

2 cups (14 oz/440 g) yellow split mung beans (see Hint)

1 cup (8 oz/250 g) sugar

3 tablespoons sesame seeds, lightly toasted (see Hint, page 55)

Place beans in a medium pot or saucepan and add water to cover. Bring to a boil, reduce heat and simmer until tender, about 30 minutes. Drain well, but do not rinse. Let cool slightly, then transfer to a food processor and puree coarsely, or mash in pan using a potato masher.

Return puree to pot and stir in sugar. Cook over very low heat, stirring or mashing until puree becomes rather dry and pulls away from pan into a ball, about 5–10 minutes.

Lightly moisten a large bowl or mold with water. Add cooked puree and press compactly into bowl or mold. Turn out and sprinkle with sesame seeds.

Serves 8

Note: This dish is popular holiday fare and is especially good as a snack served with hot jasmine tea.

Hint: Dried mung beans—either split yellow or whole green—are available at Asian stores and some natural foods stores; at Indian markets split mung beans are known as moong dal, and whole beans are known as sabat moong.

If using whole green mung beans, soak in water for several hours, then rinse well to remove the outer green shell, then proceed as above.

Ingredients

1/3 **cup (3 fl oz/90 ml) freshly squeezed lemon or lime juice**

1/3 **cup (3 fl oz/90 ml) Sugar Syrup (below), plus more (to taste) if required**

pinch of salt (optional)

ice cubes

about 1 cup (8 fl oz/250 ml) soda water or water

Fresh lemon or lime soda
Nuoc chanh da/soda chanh

In a glass, combine lime juice, sugar syrup and salt, if using. Pour into a glass tumbler packed with ice. Add soda water to fill and add more sugar syrup to taste, if desired.

Serves 1–2

Ingredients

1 cup (8 oz/250 g) sugar

1 cup (8 fl oz/250 ml) water

Sugar syrup
Nuoc duong

In a medium saucepan, combine sugar and water. Cook over low heat, stirring until sugar dissolves. Stop stirring, increase heat to high and bring to a boil. Cook for 3 minutes without stirring. To prevent syrup from crystallizing, brush pan side with cold water. Remove from heat and let cool completely. Pour into a jar, cover, and refrigerate indefinitely.

Makes 1 1/4 cups (10 fl oz/300 ml)

Variation: Vanilla sugar syrup Add 1 vanilla bean, split lengthwise, to sugar syrup after removing it from heat. Alternatively, stir in 1/4 teaspoon vanilla extract (essence).

Lemongrass tea
Che sa/tra sa

Ingredients

3 green shoots (leaves) lemongrass (see Hint)

about 1 cup (8 fl oz/250 ml) boiling water

Crush lemongrass shoots and place into mug or large teacup. Alternatively, wrap leaves attractively into a bunch, tying them together with a leaf. Pour boiling water over, cover, and let steep for 2–3 minutes. Leave lemongrass in cup while drinking.

Serves 1

Hint: Lemongrass tea is made from the green shoot-like leaves at the top of the plant, not the white bulbous base used in cooking. If fresh lemongrass is unavailable, look for dried lemongrass. Use frugally.

Variation: Iced lemongrass tea (Che sa da/Tra sa da) Steep tea for 5 minutes, let cool, then pour over ice. Add Sugar Syrup (page 108) to taste.

Soy milk
Sua dau nanh

Ingredients

⅓ cup (2 oz/60 g) dried yellow soybeans

8 cups (64 fl oz/2 L) warm water

½ cup (4 fl oz/125 ml) Vanilla Sugar Syrup (page 108) or to taste

Rinse and pick over soybeans. Put soybeans in a medium bowl and add warm water. Soak overnight, then drain, reserving soaking water. Rinse beans briskly under cold running water and drain again. In a blender (a food processor does not work well here), combine beans and about ¾ cup (6 fl oz/180 ml) of soaking water; puree. Add remaining soaking water, then strain through several layers of cheesecloth (muslin). In a medium saucepan, bring strained liquid to a boil, reduce heat to low and simmer for 10 minutes. Remove from heat and add vanilla sugar syrup, plus more to taste if desired. Let cool, then pour over ice and serve. Soy milk is best drunk freshly made.

Serves 6

Ingredients

3–4 heaping teaspoons very finely ground espresso-roast coffee

⅓ cup (3 fl oz/90 ml) boiling water

ice cubes

sugar to taste

Vietnamese iced coffee
Ca-phe den da

Remove top filter or inner screen from a Vietnamese coffee filter by unscrewing it counterclockwise (anticlockwise). (Some versions attach with a clip or a pressure spring. See Note.) Fill fully with coffee, pat to compress, and secure filter. Set coffee filter atop a small bistro glass and add boiling water. Cover with top lid to retain heat. The coffee will slowly drip through. Meanwhile, fill a small water glass with crushed ice or ice cubes.

When coffee has fully dripped through, about 3 minutes, remove top lid of filter and invert it as a saucer to catch any remaining drips. Remove coffee filter and place it atop inverted lid. Pour coffee over ice in glass. If desired, sweeten with sugar to taste.

Serves 1

Note: If a Vietnamese coffee filter is unavailable, a French-press coffeepot is a close equivalent.

Hint: If coffee drips too quickly, it is either because the coffee grind is too coarse or because the filter has not been packed tightly with sufficient coffee. Conversely, over-packed coffee may not drip at all.

Variations: With sweetened milk (Ca-phe nau nong/Ca-phe nau da) Carefully pour 2 tablespoons sweetened condensed milk into a small bistro glass. It should form a single layer, and not run down sides. Place coffee filter atop, and proceed as above, allowing coffee to slowly drip into glass. The finished coffee will appear in two layers, similar to a French pousse-café. Serve hot, or pour over ice.

With cinnamon: Prepare as for iced coffee, but do not pour over ice. Sweetening with sugar or sweetened condensed milk is optional; use a cinnamon stick to stir. Leave cinnamon in coffee to further flavor it. Alternatively, sprinkle with a pinch ground cinnamon.

Ingredients

- 1 tablespoon rice vinegar or distilled white vinegar
- 2 tablespoons finely chopped brown or pink shallots (French shallots)
- 1/3 cup (3 fl oz/90 ml) coconut cream or coconut milk (page 119)
- 1/3 cup (3 fl oz/90 ml) bean sauce (bean paste) (tuong) or canned whole salted soybeans, mashed
- 1/2 fresh long red chili, seeded and finely chopped
- 2 tablespoons sugar
- 2 tablespoons peanuts, lightly toasted (see Hint, page 55) and chopped

Bean sauce
Nuoc tuong/Tuong goi cuon

In a small saucepan, combine vinegar and shallots. Bring to a boil and cook until liquid is almost all reduced. Add coconut cream and bring to a boil. Add bean sauce and cook, stirring constantly, for about 1 minute. Add chilies and sugar, and cook, stirring, until sugar is dissolved, about 2 minutes. Remove from heat and let cool. Sprinkle with peanuts and serve.

Makes about 1¼ cups (10 fl oz/300 ml)

Note: This sauce is delicious with grilled meats. It traditionally accompanies such dishes as Fresh Spring Rolls (page 38) and Sugarcane Shrimp (page 44).

Ingredients

- 1 cup (8 fl oz/250 ml) bottled fish sauce
- 1–2 fresh small to medium green or red chilies, coarsely chopped
- 1/4 cup (2 fl oz/60 ml) water
- pinch sugar

Simple fish sauce
Nuoc mam

In a small bowl, combine all ingredients and stir to blend.

Makes 1¼ cups (10 fl oz/310 ml)

Note: This sauce is best consumed on the day it is made.

Nuoc cham **sauce**

Ingredients

8 cloves garlic

4 fresh medium red chilies

½ cup (4 oz/125 g) sugar

juice of 4 limes

1 cup (8 fl oz/250 ml) fish sauce

2 cups (16 fl oz/500 ml) water

In a mortar, using a pestle, pound garlic and chilies to a paste. Add all remaining ingredients and stir until dissolved. Alternatively, combine all ingredients in a blender or food processor and puree.

Makes about 3½ cups (28 fl oz/875 ml)

Notes: This is the most ubiquitous sauce in Vietnam. Use it at the table to dip, season, or sprinkle on anything.

This sauce is best consumed on the day it is made, or the day after.

Nuoc cham nem **sauce**

Ingredients

3 cloves garlic

1 fresh long red chili, seeded

½ cup (4 fl oz/125 ml) fish sauce

¼ cup (2 fl oz/60 ml) rice vinegar or distilled white vinegar

⅔ cup (5 fl oz/160 ml) water

3–4 tablespoons sugar (to taste)

1 carrot, peeled and finely shredded or chopped

½ cup (2 oz/60 g) peeled and shredded and chopped green papaya (See Hint)

½ teaspoon ground pepper

In a mortar, using a pestle, pound garlic and chili to a paste. Stir in fish sauce, vinegar, water and sugar, and continue stirring until sugar is dissolved. Alternatively, in a blender or food processor, combine garlic, chili, fish sauce, vinegar, water and sugar; puree. Stir in shredded carrot, papaya and pepper.

Makes about 2 cups (16 fl oz/500 ml)

Note: This sauce is best consumed on the day it is made, or the day after. Serve liberally, as it complements most dishes, especially fried spring rolls. Both sauce and carrot and fruit are consumed.

Hint: If green papaya is unavailable, substitute shredded, peeled daikon (giant white radish) or jicama (yam bean). Shredded daikon smells strongly if not used within a few hours.

In Vietnam the carrot and papaya used in this recipe may be carved into flat flower forms, or alternatively cut into thin slices, ⅓-inch (1-cm) pieces.

Fermented shrimp dipping sauce

Nuoc mam tom/Nuoc mam ruoc

Ingredients

½ cup fermented shrimp paste (mam tom/mam ruoc)

2 tablespoons freshly squeezed lime juice

2 teaspoons sugar

pinch finely chopped fresh chili

In a small bowl, stir all ingredients together to make a medium-thick sauce. If necessary, add 1 teaspoon water at a time to make it just thin enough to drizzle.

Makes about ⅔ cup (5 fl oz/160 ml)

Notes: This sauce is a traditional accompaniment to both Cha Ca Fish with Turmeric (page 88) and Sizzling Coconut Crepes (page 96). Use sparingly.

Southern Vietnam's ruoc and its northern counterpart, mam tom, are both made from fermented shrimp essence, although they differ in thickness. Both are extremely pungent, and may be too powerful for most Western palates. Premium Chinese shrimp paste can also be used.

Ingredients

1 chicken, preferably a stewing (steamer) hen, whole or cut up

about 4–6 cups (32–48 oz/1–1.5 L) water

½-inch (1.2-cm) knob fresh ginger, thinly sliced

2 leeks, white part only, or 4 scallions (shallots/spring onions), including green parts

Chicken stock
Nuoc dung ga

Rinse chicken well under running water. Put in a stockpot and add cold water to just cover chicken, about 4–6 cups (1–1.5 L). Bring to a boil, uncovered, over medium heat. Skim to remove foam, then add ginger and leeks. Reduce heat to a simmer and cook until flavored, about 1½–3 hours; strain and cool. To remove fat, either chill stock until fat hardens, or gently float paper towels on top to extract fat, then discard.

Variations: Enriched meat stock (Nuoc xuong ham) Proceed as above, adding 1 pig's foot that has previously been blanched in boiling water for 1 minute, and 1 lb (500 g) cubed boneless pork shoulder or butt (leg). Optionally, add 1–2 onions, some celery leaves, 2 carrots, ½ teaspoon whole peppercorns and 1 brown or black cardamom, plus salt to taste.

Beef stock (Nuoc dung bo): For a richer stock, begin with chicken stock; alternatively use water. Proceed as with enriched meat stock, omitting pork and adding beef bones that have been browned under the broiler (grill). Add 1 lb (500 g) diced beef shank, or any cheap stewing beef. Add 2 brown or black cardamoms, or 2–3 star anise. Partially cover and simmer gently for 3–4 hours.

Quick Seafood stock (Nuoc dung bo bien): In a stockpot, combine shells of shrimp, crab or other crustaceans with weak chicken stock or water. If desired, add 1–2 onions or white portion of 1–2 leeks, some celery leaves, 2 carrots, ½ teaspoon whole peppercorns and salt to taste. Cook as described in Chicken Stock recipe above. Alternatively, the cooking liquid from raw crab in its shell makes a delicious and simple seafood stock.

Fish stock (Nuoc dung ca): Fish stock is made from the skin, bones and heads of fish. If using oily fish, such as salmon or mackerel, do not use heads and skin. In a stockpot, place fish pieces, 1–2 onions or white portion of 1–2 leeks, celery leaves, 2 carrots, ½ teaspoon whole peppercorns and salt to taste. Add enough weak chicken stock or cold water to cover. Fish stock should be brought only to a low boil, then simmered for 20 minutes, or it may turn bitter.

Note: Stock may be kept in the refrigerator for 2–3 days, or frozen.

Coconut cream, milk and water

Nuoc cot dua/Sua dua/Nuoc dua

Ingredients

1 fresh coconut

Choose a good-quality coconut by shaking it to see if it is full of water. If there is none present, discard coconut. If the coconut flesh has spoiled or dried, it will rattle slightly. Hold coconut in your hand, resting it in a heavy tea towel, and use a large knife or small machete to crack coconut by scoring lightly across its circumference. Strike sharply with knife to crack shell. Insert the blade into the crack to pry apart. Take extra care lest you cut your hand. Alternatively, drop coconut onto a hard concrete surface, or use a hammer. Use a small hand grater to scrape out coconut meat in shreds. Alternatively, place shells in a moderate oven for 15–20 minutes. The flesh will shrink slightly, facilitating removal of the coconut matter. Grate in a food processor.

Put grated coconut in a tea towel and wring it tightly, or put it in a sieve and press it firmly with the back of a large spoon to extract cream; reserve liquid. A chinois sieve, or China cap, works well here.

Add just enough warm or hot water to cover shredded coconut, and press it again to extract thick coconut milk. Repeat again to extract thin coconut milk.

Canned coconut milk or cream can be substituted for fresh. Make sure not to use sweetened coconut milk or cream. Generally speaking, the less the can shakes, the richer the coconut milk. However, just before using, take care not to shake can. Open carefully and spoon off richest portion (refrigeration facilitates this step) to separate it from the thinner coconut milk.

The liquid sloshing inside the coconut is coconut water, not to be confused with its milk or cream. A young coconut with immature flesh holds the greatest volume of coconut water, but only a fully mature coconut should be used for extracting cream or milk from grated meat.

Ingredients

3–6 cups uncooked long-grain rice,
preferably jasmine

Step-by-step
steamed **rice**

Com

1. Rinse rice in several changes of water until water runs clear, but do not overwork rice, lest grains break. Drain.

2. Place rice in a deep, medium to large, heavy-based saucepan or pot with a tight-fitting lid. Fill with just enough water to cover rice by 1 inch (2.5 cm). (Traditionally, cooks measured by placing their index finger on top of the rice and adding enough water to come to the first joint.) Bring to a boil, uncovered, over high heat and cook until craters form in rice. Immediately cover tightly and reduce heat; simmer until tender, about 20 minutes. Do not lift lid during cooking.

3. Use a rice paddle to fluff up rice and loosen grains.

Makes 6–12 cups

Note: Though commonly referred to as "steamed rice," this rice is actually boiled.

1

2

3

Step-by-step
thin flat **omelets**
Trung trang mong

Ingredients

1–2 eggs

1 tablespoon water

pinch sugar

pinch salt (optional)

vegetable oil cooking

1. Using a fork, beat egg(s)—you can use one egg or two to make a single omelet—until blended. Add 1 tablespoon water and sugar, and salt if using.

2. Heat an 8-inch (20-cm) frying pan over medium heat. Add enough oil to coat bottom. It should sizzle if hit with a drop of water. Pour beaten egg into pan, lifting pan to tilt it quickly to allow egg to spread out evenly. Reduce heat to low and cook just until set, about 30 seconds.

3. Carefully flip over omelet and cook a few seconds on second side. It should be firm and not runny. Transfer to a plate to cool.

Cooked omelets, either stacked flat or rolled, can be wrapped tightly in plastic wrap and refrigerated for up to 2 days.

Makes 1 omelet

Hint: Use whole omelets to wrap food. For omelet strips, loosely roll 2 or 3 cooked omelets into a cylinder, then cut crosswise into strips.

Note: Thin omelets are used in a large number of dishes, such as Pork Omelet Roll (page 48), and as a substitute for crepes in Sizzling Coconut Crepes (page 96). Alternatively, simply roll and thinly slice and use as a garnish to fried rice and various salads.

1

2

3

Glossary

Bananas (chuoi) Both dwarf (ladies' finger/sugar) bananas, as well as medium-sized Cavendish, are eaten in Vietnam. Generally speaking, the smaller the banana the sweeter it is. Green bananas are thinly sliced through the skin and served as an astringent complement.

Bread rolls (banh mi) Crisp French-style rolls have long been a mainstay in Vietnam. Generally slightly shorter and narrower than a baguette and akin to a batard, these are often eaten as a sandwich filled with thin slices of Silky Pork Sausage (page 49) or meatball stew, or as an accompaniment to dishes like Beef Braised in Rice Wine (page 86).

Cassava (manioc) starch (flour) See tapioca.

Chili powder, Asian (ot bot) Made from long dried chilies, Asian chili powder, as used in Vietnam and Southeast Asia, is not is not as piquant as cayenne pepper. It is not the same as Mexican chili powder, which is a combination of herbs and spices.

Cilantro (fresh coriander) (rau mui/rau ngo) The fresh leaf, stem and root of the coriander plant. Both stems and leaves are commonly chopped and added to food, and sprigs are used as garnish and served at the table as an accompaniment or table green. Not to be confused with coriander seed. Also known as Chinese parsley.

Coconut milk and cream (nuoc dua/nuoc cot dua) Coconut cream is the first—and richest—pressing from freshly grated coconut; coconut milk is thinner.

Coconut water (nuoc dua tuoi) The clear, watery liquid inside a coconut, preferably from young coconuts. It is very different from coconut milk, which is extracted from the flesh.

Cornstarch (cornflour) (bot ngo) Although not as popular in the Vietnamese kitchen as arrowroot—primarily because it is more expensive (the opposite to the West)—cornstarch is generally interchangeable. It must be boiled to remove its starchy taste. Use cornstarch to dredge (lightly coat) meat prior to frying

Fish sauce (nuoc mam) An important source of protein and salt in the Vietnamese diet, and much more common than soy sauce. Pure fish sauce is known as nuoc mam nguyen chat, while the first-pressing premium grade is nuoc mam nhi. Cheaper grades are nuoc mam thuong (regular fish sauce) and nuoc mam kho (for cooking). Unfortunately, these terms are seldom employed on sauce sold overseas. Let price be your guiding rule. Save premium fish sauces for the table, with cheaper varieties relegated to cooking. While the tiny southern island of Phu Quoc is renowned as one source of the country's most prestigious fish sauces, some brands prominently displaying geographic names may actually be made in Thailand or Hong Kong. Read the label closely. Avoid bottles that list "hydrolyzed protein" as an ingredient, as it indicates chemical manufacture. Although labels may boast names suggesting crabs, shrimp, and other seafood, these have nothing to do with the bottles' contents. Asian cookbooks commonly state that fish sauce lasts indefinitely, but this has more to do with its copious and constant use there, rather than true longevity. Once opened, use within 1 month at room temperature, or refrigerate for up to 6 months. After that, the flavor deteriorates. (See also Ingredients, page 20.)

Five-spice powder (ngu vi huong) A combination of ground star anise (the taste of which dominates), plus fennel seeds, cassia or cinnamon, cloves, and black or Sichuan pepper. It is available from Asian markets and some supermarkets.

Garlic (toi) Fresh garlic ensures better flavor than pastes and dried flakes or powders. Generally, the smaller the bulbs, the stronger the flavor. The standard size of garlic cloves used in this book is large, about the size of an almond.

Julienne To cut into long, thin strips.

Lemon and lime leaves (chanh/la chanh) Fresh leaves from these two citrus trees are interspersed on skewers with grilled meat. Substitute with kaffir lime leaves.

Manioc (cassava) starch (flour) See tapioca.

Milk, sweetened condensed (sua dac co duong) Popular throughout Southeast Asia, this is commonly used to sweeten tea and coffee, as well as desserts like Sweet Black Bean Soup (page 104). Do not substitute evaporated milk, which is neither thick nor sweetened.

Oil (dau an/dau nau) Sunflower, corn, peanut and soybean oils are all popular in Vietnam. Despite their long French colonization, Vietnamese do not cook with olive oil. Traditionally, they use fat and lard.

Piper leaf (la lot) Mild-tasting piper leaves are incorrectly identified both as "pepper leaf" and, more commonly, "beetle leaf." There exists a similarly shaped, but larger and less shiny leaf, known as the true "beetle" or "pepper" leaf. It is in the same piper family, but distinctly different, as its taste is hot and peppery; and the leaf is wrapped around sliced betelnut seed, which is the Asian equivalent of chewing tobacco. The similarity of the two leaves leads to all sorts of confusion, hence the common misappropriation of its name.

Rau song The generic term for herbs, as in greens.

Rice Long-grain white Jasmine is the standard table rice of Vietnam, although chalky-looking sticky or glutinous rice is also popular—especially in desserts. These two varieties are not interchangeable, and require different cooking techniques.

Rice alcohol (ruou gao) A mild version of this is made by fermenting black sticky rice; it resembles cooked rice. A more pungent version comes as a neutral spirit, sold in bottles. Substitute with vodka.

Rice, ground (thinh) Ground rice grain is made from toasting raw grains of sticky rice and then grinding it coarsely with a stone mortar and pestle. It is added for texture. Do not confuse with generic rice starch. (See also page 44.)

Rice wine (nuoc ruou nep/ruou can) Made from sticky (glutinous) rice, rice wine may be either dry or sweet. Substitute dry or sweet sherry. Sweet rice wine makes a delicious chilled aperitif.

Shallots (french shallots), fried or dried (hanh kho chao ron) Crisply fried shallots (often blended with scallions) are available packaged in Asian markets. They are convenient garnishes for soups and salads and store well for months. Also labeled "fried red onion."

Shrimp sauce (mam tom/mam ruoc) Ruoc (from the south of Vietnam) and mam tom (from the north) differ in thickness but both are extremely pungent. They are available from Asian markets. (See also Ingredients, page 21.)

Simmer A low to moderate cooking temperature so that liquid barely quivers, just below the boiling point. A common cooking mistake is to "simmer" at too low a temperature, resulting in under-cooked meat and vegetables.

Soy sauce (xi dau) In Vietnam, this condiment is used primarily in Chinese dishes or in vegetarian offerings, when fish sauce is inappropriate. It is rarely served at the table, except to foreigners, whom Vietnamese presume will dislike fish sauce.

Tapioca starch (flour) (bot san cu/bot san day) Made from the cassava, or manioc, tuber, this flour is primarily used to blend with sticky (glutinous) rice starch in some cakes and sweet drinks, and to bind ground meat, less for thickening sauces.

Vinegar (dam trang) The principal vinegar used in Vietnam is white rice vinegar. Substitute with distilled white vinegar, coconut vinegar, or white wine vinegar, but note that Western vinegars have a higher acidic content and may need diluting. If using Japanese rice vinegar, ensure it is not sweetened with mirin.

Index

Guide to weights and measures

The conversions given in the recipes in this book are approximate. Whichever system you use, remember to follow it consistently, thereby ensuring that the proportions are consistent throughout a recipe.

WEIGHTS

Imperial	Metric
⅓ oz	10 g
½ oz	15 g
¾ oz	20 g
1 oz	30 g
2 oz	60 g
3 oz	90 g
4 oz (¼ lb)	125 g
5 oz (⅓ lb)	150 g
6 oz	180 g
7 oz	220 g
8 oz (½ lb)	250 g
9 oz	280 g
10 oz	300 g
11 oz	330 g
12 oz (¾ lb)	375 g
16 oz (1 lb)	500 g
2 lb	1 kg
3 lb	1.5 kg
4 lb	2 kg

VOLUME

Imperial	Metric	Cup
1 fl oz	30 ml	
2 fl oz	60 ml	¼
3 fl oz	90 ml	⅓
4 fl oz	125 ml	½
5 fl oz	150 ml	⅔
6 fl oz	180 ml	¾
8 fl oz	250 ml	1
10 fl oz	300 ml	1¼
12 fl oz	375 ml	1½
13 fl oz	400 ml	1⅔
14 fl oz	440 ml	1¾
16 fl oz	500 ml	2
24 fl oz	750 ml	3
32 fl oz	1 L	4

USEFUL CONVERSIONS

¼ teaspoon	1.25 ml
½ teaspoon	2.5 ml
1 teaspoon	5 ml
1 Australian tablespoon	20 ml (4 teaspoons)
1 UK/US tablespoon	15 ml (3 teaspoons)

OVEN TEMPERATURE GUIDE

The Celsius (°C) and Fahrenheit (°F) temperatures in this chart apply to most electric ovens. Decrease by 25°F (10°C) for a gas oven or refer to the manufacturer's temperature guide. For temperatures below 325°F (160°C), do not decrease the given temperature.

Oven description	°C	°F	Gas Mark
Cool	110	225	¼
	130	250	½
Very slow	140	275	1
	150	300	2
Slow	170	325	3
Moderate	180	350	4
	190	375	5
Moderately Hot	200	400	6
Fairly Hot	220	425	7
Hot	230	450	8
Very Hot	240	475	9
Extremely Hot	250	500	10